The Clockwork Muse

THE
CLOCKWORK
Muse

A PRACTICAL GUIDE TO WRITING
THESES, DISSERTATIONS, AND BOOKS

EVIATAR ZERUBAVEL

HARVARD UNIVERSITY PRESS

Cambridge, Massachusetts, and London, England 1999

Library of Congress Cataloging-in-Publication Data

Zerubavel, Eviatar.
The clockwork muse : a practical guide to writing theses,
dissertations, and books / Eviatar Zerubavel.
p.   cm.
Includes bibliographical references (p.   ) and index.
ISBN 0-674-13585-7 (cloth : alk. paper). —
ISBN 0-674-13586-5 (paper : alk. paper)
1. Authorship.   2. Dissertations, Academic—Authorship.
I. Title.
PN145.Z47   1999
808'.02—dc21   98-39775

Designed by Gwen Nefsky Frankfeldt

To Noga,
a writer I love and admire

Contents

Acknowledgments

A number of people deserve my deep appreciation and gratitude for their considerable efforts in helping me make this book much better than it would have been without them. I owe special thanks, in this regard, to Yael Zerubavel, Ruth Simpson, Dan Ryan, Nicole Isaacson, Marlie Wasserman, and my production editor Kate Brick for having read my manuscript, and wish to acknowledge how much I benefited from the extensive feedback they gave me. I would also like to thank Nira Granott for having been the first person who took my general approach to writing seriously enough to encourage me to write this book, and my editor Michael Aronson for expressing the enthusiasm necessary to help me bring it to completion. I dedicate this book to my daughter Noga, a writer whom I will always love and admire.

The Clockwork Muse

The Clockwork Muse

It is almost impossible to live in the modern world and not have to write. This is particularly true if you are a student, an administrator, or a scholar, not to mention a professional writer.

Unfortunately, writing is an activity that tends to evoke a considerable amount of anxiety, often resulting in the paralytic condition commonly known as a "writer's block." This is especially true if you are working on long projects such as a grant proposal, an annual report, or a senior thesis, not to mention a doctoral dissertation or a book.

Such anxiety, unfortunately, does not necessarily go away as you gain more professional experience as a writer. Even seasoned writers still dread having to start from scratch on a new book, knowing that they are probably several years away from completion. This situation is even more daunting, of course, for relatively inexperienced writers who are just about to launch their first major project.

While recognizing that such anxiety may very well be an inevitable part of producing theses, dissertations, and books, I nevertheless try to offer prospective writers various strategies of coping with this anxiety in the most effective manner in this book. Thus, I specifically address difficult psychological problems such as having to deal with pressure and timidity as well as procrastination and burnout. I likewise try to offer writers practical solutions to common logistic problems such as how to meet deadlines, how to find the time to write even in extremely demanding job situations, and how to integrate their writing into the rest of their personal involvements and social commitments so as to maintain a more balanced life.

The book builds on the fundamental premise that, unless we learn how to overcome problems having to do with *how* we write, we may never be able to focus on what we actually want to write about. As such, it dwells specifically on the "procedural" aspects of the process of producing a manuscript. Hence its particular concern with our need to develop better work habits (and, consequently, to also regard "writer's block" and procrastination as technical rather than strictly psychological problems).

Good work habits include effective *planning,* perhaps the key to gaining better control over one's writing. In this book I present a set of strategies for planning your writing, both generally and at the level of any particular project. These strategies revolve around a particular aspect of the writing process that is rarely explicitly addressed in our training as writers, namely the way in which it is temporally organized. As I shall demonstrate by focusing specifically on this neglected dimension of our life as writers, an effective temporal organization of our writing can help make it far less stressful and thus help us accomplish personal and professional goals we might otherwise consider totally out of our reach.

The key to an effective temporal organization of our writing lies in one of the most remarkable inventions of Western civilization, namely the *time schedule*. Originally introduced

. . . .

𝓘t is methodicalness and routinization that help us produce theses, dissertations, and books. And it is the time schedule and the timetable that help us bring them into our writing.

. . . .

fifteen centuries ago by an Italian monk as part of a larger attempt to routinize and thereby systematize daily monastic life, the schedule has clearly become one of the cornerstones of modern life.[1] And although unlike Saint Benedict himself I do not regard routinization as an ideal principle for organizing our lives in general (and would therefore never recommend applying it, for example, to such activities as listening to music or making love), I do regard it as one of the most effective means of organizing our writing—a process that, for many of us, may never yield a completed product unless structured methodically. It is methodicalness and routinization, in other words, that help us produce theses, dissertations, and books. And it is the time schedule, along with its functional cousin the *timetable,* that helps us bring them into our writing.

Needless to say, there is an inherent tension between routine and spontaneity, and writing in accordance with schedules and timetables rather than when you simply "get to it" certainly also makes it much less spontaneous.[2] The very idea of establishing regular writing times clearly contrasts with our vision of writing (or engaging in any other creative activity) only when "inspired." Submitting yourself in a self-disciplined manner to temporal routines certainly undermines the common Romantic image of the bohemian writer who forgoes structure in order to accommodate essentially unscheduled outbursts of creative energy.

A careful examination of actual writers' work habits, however, strongly suggests that such an image is by and large a myth. Very few writers actually sit down to write only when they feel particularly inspired. Furthermore, it is a rather dangerous myth, since it might lead you to willingly relinquish much of the control you can have over your writing by opting to rely on some mysterious and rather capricious "muse" that you may actually encounter perhaps a couple of times a year. While you can sometimes afford to do so when working on a short poem, a two-page essay, or an op-ed piece, waiting to be struck by inspiration is obviously somewhat impractical when you are trying to produce a full-fledged master's thesis, doctoral dissertation, or book. Such projects require numerous writing sessions, and if those were to take place only when you actually feel like writing, they might never be completed at all. Deromanticizing the writing process is therefore of utmost importance to any writer in the making, and it basically challenges the way we traditionally associate creativity with structurelessness and spontaneity.

Writing in accordance with a time schedule offers us considerable advantages. Perhaps most important, it makes it a lot easier for us to establish a routine that ensures that we would indeed get to write. As anyone who exercises or plays the piano on a regular basis knows, scheduled routines make it much easier to "get to" do things we might otherwise leave out of our daily lives altogether. If you cannot "find the time"

By allotting to writing a specific daily or weekly time slot, a schedule ensures that you will get to do it on a regular basis.

to write, you will most likely discover that, by establishing a regular weekly schedule that includes just forty-five minutes of writing every Tuesday and Friday morning, for example, you will inevitably manage to get some writing done! By allotting to writing a specific (daily or weekly) time slot, a schedule ensures that you will indeed get to do it on a regular basis.

Furthermore, scheduling helps us integrate our writing much more effectively into the rest of our life. As a mathematically manipulable variable,[3] time is a perfect medium for establishing priorities, and involvements that are more important to us are usually also those for which we allow more time. (The number of hours children spend every week in math and art classes, for example, is indicative of the relative respect those two subjects seem to command in the school curriculum.)[4] In fact, it is hard to imagine a more effective way of systematically regulating our various involvements in life. If writing that book or dissertation is indeed so much more important to you than watching television or reading the newspaper, for example, you can certainly make sure, through the use of a schedule, that you actually allow it much more time than you allow the latter. By the same token, if you want to ensure that you do not spend on your writing more time than you do on playing with your children, you can quite easily arrange that with the help of a schedule.

Following a schedule, in short, helps us allocate our various involvements in the exact proportions we desire and thereby strike an optimal balance among them.[5] It also allows us to organize those involvements in accordance with a predetermined structure of priorities rather than be at the mercy of our constantly changing whims.

In fact, by making it easier for us to actually disentangle our various daily and weekly activities from one another (thus ensuring that what we normally do on Wednesday mornings, for example, would never conflict with what we usually do on Thursday afternoons),[6] scheduling also allows us to be more comfortably involved in each of them without feeling the pressure from our involvements in the others. A schedule helps a busy professor protect her highly treasured writing time from the competing demands of her various teaching and administrative duties, not to mention those involved in being a mother and a wife. It likewise helps a student protect the time he needs to spend on writing his doctoral dissertation from the competing demands of friends, various hobbies, and a part-time job. In fact, as John Barth reminds us, it even helps writers engage in somewhat different kinds of writing: "Four mornings a week . . . [I] make up and set down my stories in a pleasant white house in the city of Baltimore . . . [On] Thursday evenings my wife and I drive across the Chesapeake Bay Bridge to a pleasant red house on Langford Creek . . . where on Friday mornings . . . I refresh my head with some other sort of sentence-making, preferably nonfiction."[7]

Yet scheduling also helps ensure that our involvement in writing would not somehow take over the rest of our life. In providing our writing with some structure (and therefore also some limits), it helps us make sure that we would also get to do on a regular basis other things besides just writing and thereby lead more well-rounded, balanced lives. Regular writing schedules, for example, can help us maintain a relatively solid family and social life when we write. After all, like many other addictive involvements, writing often makes us somewhat difficult to be around (not to mention live with) from our roommates', partners', children's, or friends' standpoint. It can also make it quite difficult for many writers to hold a steady job. Writing in accordance with a regular schedule with some built-in "brakes" can help alleviate such problems to some extent.

Imposing a regular temporal structure with certain limits on our writing also helps protect us from various health problems generated by unstructured living. When we are deeply engrossed in our writing, we often tend to forgo not only a more balanced family and social life but also regular eating and sleeping patterns in order to accommodate our intense outbursts of creative energy. While very romantic, such a "manic" work style can rarely be sustained, making it somewhat impractical for anyone who is trying to write a thesis, a dissertation, or a book.

Furthermore, such intense outbursts of creativity are very

often followed by far less romantic hangover periods. Writing in accordance with a schedule with some built-in limits thus makes it somewhat easier to avoid writers' burnout.

Scheduling also enhances the actual pleasure of writing by making it more comfortable. By providing this essentially amorphous process with some structure, carefully designed timetables help to make it somewhat more predictable and thus considerably less intimidating. By allowing us to comfortably "pace" ourselves when we write, they also help reduce the pressure we usually associate with this process as well as keep us from procrastinating.

My own awareness of a useful link between scheduling and writing goes back to the spring of 1976, when I was about to begin writing my doctoral dissertation, a 300-page document I was absolutely determined to complete within the few remaining months before I would become a father and start my first full-time job—both of which, I rightly suspected, would leave me very little time for any intensive writing. The seeds of the system I present here were sown that spring, as I began to experiment with various schedules and timetables that would help me accomplish my goal in an effective yet comfortable manner. The results of those early experiments were quite promising. Not only did I manage to complete my dissertation that summer, I actually finished writing it a few weeks ahead of schedule!

The system I developed turned out to be of even greater help to me during the four following years, when I was working full-time on a rather demanding research job that was totally unrelated to my own research. I had two options of dealing with that situation. One was to be "realistic" and stop trying to work on my own writing, which was indeed what some of my colleagues chose to do. The other was to somehow develop my own writing agenda and stubbornly stick to it despite the constant pressure and demands of my job. Having chosen the latter, I once again found the solution in various schedules and timetables that helped me rewrite my dissertation as a book as well as complete eight journal articles and a second book during those four years while still keeping my job.

Not only did the system I developed as a result of those experiments with scheduling work so well for me during those early years of my professional career, it also became the foundation for the way I have come to organize my writing ever since then. During the twenty-one years that have passed since I finished my dissertation, I have managed to complete seven single-authored books and more than twenty journal articles, all planned and written in accordance with it. And as my various editors and publishers have come to learn, when I sign an advance contract committing myself to complete a manuscript by a certain deadline, they can fully count on it in their own plans, which is not something one usually takes for granted in the somewhat unpredictable world of publishing.

I should also add that I have had a full-time job and taken only one sabbatical (or any other) leave during those twenty-one years, and have taken an equal share in raising two children. Furthermore, I am actually a rather slow writer, yet one who has come to learn that being slow *but steady* at the level of any single workday allows me to become quite prolific at the level of my entire lifetime.

Although originally developed for my own use, the system

I present here is something that might also be useful to those like the many students, colleagues, and friends I have watched throughout the years giving up somewhere along the way and never completing the very promising manuscripts they had started to write. Having taught for almost twenty years and served as director of three graduate programs (at Columbia, Stony Brook, and currently at Rutgers), I have watched many bright students fail to complete their theses or doctoral dissertations while far less gifted yet highly organized and disciplined ones did, and have come to learn that, in writing as in other professional activities, accomplishment has to do with more than just ability.

As anyone who has ever watched musicians or gymnasts practice a difficult passage or routine over and over again knows, it is never "talent" alone that produces excellence.[8] Good work habits and perseverance usually separate those who manage to complete their manuscripts from those who do not.

It is my strong wish to help people realize their full potential as writers that has led me over the past fifteen years to offer advice and various tips to students, colleagues, and friends who got stuck at different stages of their theses, dissertations, or books and help them bring their work to completion. I have also conducted special writing workshops for students, many of whom later told me that my advice on scheduling helped them overcome writer's blocks and other major difficulties they encountered when working on their theses and dissertations. Indeed, it is their often-expressed complaint about the almost total lack of attention paid to such matters throughout their professional training that has pushed me to write this book.

Although the system I present here obviously may not be to everyone's liking (especially to people who vehemently dislike routine and for whom the very notion of a "clockwork muse" may therefore sound somewhat oxymoronic), it can certainly help those who feel even the slightest need to infuse some more structure into their writing. It can thus benefit not only people who already happen to like structure, but also many others who, although generally averse to it, nevertheless recognize that they may very well need at least some element of methodicalness and organization in order to meet their deadlines and be able to eventually complete long-term projects such as dissertations and books. And even people who may not normally like plans and agendas can nonetheless benefit from the considerable relief from both pressure and anxiety usually enjoyed by those who are willing to commit to them.

Using the system I present here, I should add, need not involve having to ultimately choose between all or nothing. There are numerous possible ways of scheduling your writing, any single one of which may very well suit your particular lifestyle and temperament better than others. What I offer here is a general framework for thinking about the temporal organization of your writing. Such a framework obviously needs to be modified to meet your particular needs, and you are therefore encouraged to further improvise on its general thematic principles and thus generate truly "customized" writing schedules and timetables that would suit you best.

Finally, let me also add that, despite its repeated use of various "time-management" techniques, this book has actually very little to do with the modern utilitarian quest for greater speed.[9] Unlike so many "how to" manuals grounded in Frederick Taylor's general philosophy of scientific management, it is not primarily designed to offer writers advice on how to become more "efficient" and does not include any practical tips on how to avoid "wasting" precious minutes or how to write a thesis in two weeks. In fact, *perseverance* is much more important than sheer speed in getting writers to actually complete their projects, which is why I have always

THE TORTOISE AND THE HARE

A hare was continually poking fun at a tortoise because of the slowness of his pace. The tortoise tried not to be annoyed by the jeers of the hare, but one day in the presence of the other animals he was goaded into challenging the hare to a foot race . . . Almost before you could say "scat" the hare was out of sight. The tortoise plodded along at his usual unhurried pace. After a time the hare stopped to wait for the tortoise to come along. He waited for a long, long time until he began to get sleepy. "I'll just take a quick nap here in this soft grass, and then in the cool of the day I'll finish the race." So he lay down and closed his eyes. Meanwhile, the tortoise plodded on. He passed the sleeping hare, and was approaching the finish line when the hare awoke with a start. It was too late to save the race. Much ashamed, he crept away while all the animals at the finish line acclaimed the winner.

Aesop's Fables
(New York: Grosset & Dunlap, 1947), pp. 34–35

liked so much Aesop's classic fable about the tortoise and the hare. Indeed, although hares are usually much more successful in churning out papers and short reports, it is often slow-but-steady tortoises who actually manage to complete theses, dissertations, and books.

The Writing Schedule

Scheduling presupposes regularity,[1] and organizing your writing in accordance with schedules and timetables involves establishing some fixed writing times. That means writing between certain hours and on certain days of the week on a regular, routine basis rather than at random.

Establishing new routines is not an easy task and usually requires a lot of effort. Once we manage to establish them, however, they soon become "second nature" habits that we then take for granted. What you need, therefore, is to establish a writing routine that will seem as natural to you as getting dressed or brushing your teeth every morning.

Setting Priorities

The first step you need to take in order to establish a regular writing routine that would actually work is to try to create a comfortable fit between your writing and the rest of your life. In order to do that, however, you first need to decide how much time you wish, or are able, to devote to your writing on a regular basis. Since that amount is inevitably calculated (even if only implicitly) relative to the amount of time that you wish, or have, to devote to other involvements in your life (your family, job, hobbies, friends), you first need to establish the relative priority of your writing vis-a-vis all those other involvements.

The most effective framework for establishing the relative priority of your writing vis-a-vis all your other routine involvements in life is probably the week, since most of those involvements happen to be "weekly" in the sense of occurring regularly either "every Wednesday" or "twice a week."[2] It is in accordance with the week, for example, that you would normally need to adjust your regular writing schedule in order to accommodate other routine commitments such as holding your office hours, taking your daughter to her music lesson, or going to the supermarket. Designing a regular *weekly writing schedule* would most likely allow you to establish the desirable proportion between your writing and all your other routine commitments in terms of hours per week.

Especially if you have never tried it before, designing a regular weekly writing schedule may require a certain period of experimentation and adjustment. You may thus discover, for example, that, although you originally intended to devote to your writing twenty hours a week, the six hours per night that you allowed for sleeping leave you somewhat exhausted the following morning and may therefore prevent you from effectively keeping up with such a demanding work schedule for more than two days in a row. By the same token, however, it is also quite possible that, only two weeks after having designed for yourself a regular writing schedule allotting ten hours a week for your writing, you may already realize that you were a bit too conservative in your estimate and can actually devote to it four additional hours every week.

Your priorities may also change from time to time. You may thus discover that, although you once used to regard writing as a relatively minor activity in your life, you are now willing (as when you are very excited about a particular project), able (as when your children grow up and need considerably less attention), or compelled (as when you have to graduate by a certain date or are coming up for tenure) to devote much more time to it. On the other hand, having just completed a very long manuscript, you might feel somewhat burned out and wish to avoid any writing for some time. If your writing is to be at all effective, you must stay in tune with such common changes of heart and allow yourself to adjust your regular weekly writing schedule from time to time so as to accommodate them.

You may also need to design more than just a single year-round weekly writing schedule, since different parts of the year sometimes offer you different writing conditions and often are associated with different sets of priorities. This is particularly true, for example, if you happen to be a student, a schoolteacher, or a college professor, thereby having several months off every summer.

Setting our priorities, of course, is not entirely a matter of personal choice; we are all confined by various external constraints.[3] Writers taking a sabbatical leave or working as a part-time waitress, for example, may find it easier to schedule time to write than writers who have a two-month-old baby or a job that requires them to spend sixty or seventy hours a week at the office.[4] Nevertheless, we usually have much more control over our time than we are willing to admit to ourselves, and if you are seriously committed to give your writing a high priority on your schedule you can normally manage to somehow find the time to write even under extremely difficult conditions both at home and at work.

Setting your priorities, in other words, entails having to take at least some responsibility for the kind of choices you make. Taking it as a necessary first step in designing for yourself a regular writing schedule implies that you cannot complain later that you simply cannot find the time to do any writing, since you set those priorities in the first place! Most of us have much more time than we would usually like to admit to ourselves. The question, though, is how we choose to set our priorities and allocate it among our various involvements in life. Thus, if we cannot seem to find the time to write, we very often have only ourselves to blame.

The Writing Session

Having decided how much time overall you wish, or are able, to devote to your writing regularly every week, you now need to break it down into units of work. In other words, you now need to establish your actual writing sessions.

First determine the length of what you would consider to be an ideal writing session. While the length of your actual writing sessions will probably vary from your plan, it is nevertheless important that you establish what you would regard as an ideal session and try to use that knowledge when designing your regular weekly writing schedule. Although family, job, and other constraints will most likely require some compromises, you should try to identify what would constitute an ideal writing session *if* you could ever have it.

When trying to establish the optimal length of your writing sessions, be sure to take into account two major ergonomic factors: the approximate amount of time it usually takes you to get into a creative mode and the approximate amount of time you can effectively sustain such a mode and be productive. Considering the first factor, of course, ought to help you avoid scheduling writing sessions that are too short. Considering the second should likewise help preclude ones that are too long. Establishing what you would consider to be an ideal writing session certainly entails staying away from either extreme.

Writing sessions that are much too short are counterproductive—you need to allow yourself enough time to "get into" a creative mode. Unlike robots, most people do not usually simply turn on their typewriter or computer and start writing right away. As they begin a work session, some go through various elaborate routines such as sharpening their pencils, preparing a cup of coffee, checking their electronic mail, and carefully rearranging things on their desk. Many others, who may not outwardly engage in any such quasi-ritual "opening ceremonies," nevertheless still seem to need at least fifteen or twenty minutes of "warming up" at the beginning of a session before they can begin to do any serious writing. If you happen to be one of those people, scheduling your writing in thirty- or forty-five-minute blocks will be a total waste of your time and effort, since any writing you might actually get to do during such brief mini-sessions is likely to be rather ineffectual, not to mention extremely frustrating.

It is very important for you at this stage to recognize such ergonomic idiosyncrasies and take them into consideration when you design your regular weekly writing schedule. After all, if you cannot concentrate on your writing for several hours without having checked your electronic mail first, there is no point in even trying to fight that. Indeed, you may do much better if you take that into consideration: always schedule for yourself regular writing sessions that are fifteen or twenty minutes longer than you might have done otherwise, and allow yourself to begin each session by checking your electronic mail first and getting it out of your way, thereby "clearing your mind" for your actual writing.

At the same time, however, it is just as important to also take into consideration the length of your creative attention span as well as the shape of your energy level (and hence productivity) curve and try to avoid scheduling for yourself writing sessions that are much too long. In other words, you must determine the optimal length of a session during which you can maintain a consistently high level of creative attention and thus keep writing effectively. Inevitably, at some point in every session, our creativity and productivity curve peaks and begins to first flatten and then fall. If, however, you learn to recognize and even anticipate that point, you can stop writing *right before* you reach it, when "you still have your juice," as Ernest Hemingway so aptly put it,[5] and can thus end your session with an upbeat sense of accomplishment rather than defeat. After all, once you go past that critical point, the marginal utility of any additional minute of writing you might get to do may actually turn out to be not only negligible but even negative! For example, if your optimal writing session is about three hours long yet you regularly schedule your writing in five-hour stretches, you are likely to find the last two hours to be a most unfulfilling and therefore frustrating waste of effort, at the end of which you will probably leave your desk feeling compelled to rewrite everything you did during those two hours. Longer is not always better, and in order to maximize your creativity and productivity you must therefore learn when to stop writing.

Note, in this regard, that our creative attention span as well as energy level and productivity curve usually vary from one writer to another. In fact, they very often also change at different points in our life. The writing sessions I can effectively manage now, as I approach fifty, are considerably shorter than the ones I used to be able to manage when I was in my twenties and early thirties. Furthermore, as John Irving suggests, they may very well change even at different stages in the life of a given project: "When I'm beginning a book, I can't work more than two or three hours a day . . . Then there's the middle of a book. I can work eight, nine, twelve hours then . . . Then when the time to finish the book comes, it's back to those two and three hour days."[6] At any given period, however, they are likely to be relatively constant and thus highly predictable, which means that you can build them quite confidently into your regular writing schedule.

Given all this, it is very important that you experiment to determine what would constitute an optimal writing session *for you.* The fact that someone else may be able to write quite effectively for nine straight hours is of absolutely no relevance if *you* cannot do so. Thus, if you still have no idea what your actual creative attention span is and what your energy level and productivity curve as a writer looks like, it may be worth your while to devote some time to finding that out, so as to ensure that the regular weekly writing schedule you end up designing for yourself is based on sessions that are indeed the most appropriate ones for you.

A Time to Write

Now that you have established the amount of time you are willing or able to devote to your writing and have broken it

> *Just as you optimize your other writing conditions, learn to identify the best times for your writing.*

down into actual work sessions, you can proceed to consider *when* you would like to write. Just as you try to optimize your other writing conditions by deciding where to place your desk or which particular word-processing software to use, you also need to identify the best times for your writing.

Evidently adhering to some notion of a "clockwork muse," most writers seem to have regular writing times: some are defined as vaguely as "two or three hours every morning" (Henry Miller, Gore Vidal), "every weekday morning" (John Updike), "on afternoons" (William Styron), or "at night" (Cynthia Ozick); some as specifically as "every morning until two in the afternoon" (Mario Vargas Llosa, John Dos Passos), "between 8:30 A.M. and 12:30 P.M." (Carlos Fuentes), "from 5:30 until noon" (John Grisham), or "from 6:30 until 12:30 or 1:30 in the afternoon" (Maya Angelou).[7] While the actual time slots they seem to favor obviously vary from one writer to another, most of them nevertheless have pretty regular writing times.

In order to design for yourself the best possible writing schedule based on such times, however, you first need to find out when you are most as well as least likely to be at your very best as a writer. In other words, you need to identify the particular times of day and days of the week on which you tend to be most as well as least creative and productive. This may require, of course, some serious experimenting over several weeks or even months. You may notice, for example, that

· ·

Keeping track of your effectiveness as a writer

Day	Hours	Comments
Monday	8:30–11:30 A.M.	"Monday blues." Found it somewhat difficult to "pick up" again and regain my momentum following the weekend.
Monday	9:00–10:00 P.M.	Very focused and energetic, but the session was much too short.
Tuesday	1:30–5:00 P.M.	Somewhat sluggish and sleepy. Not very creative. Came out feeling quite frustrated.
Wednesday	9:00 A.M.–1:00 P.M.	Great concentration. Very productive. A perfect session!
Thursday	9:30–11:00 A.M.	Much too short. Took almost an hour just to "warm up."
Friday	9:00 A.M.–3:00 P.M.	Much too long. Energy level dropped quite dramatically around 1:00.

· ·

you happen to be one of those people who are usually not too productive on Friday afternoons or Monday mornings.[8] Or you may find out that you are one of those "morning persons" who can only write effectively in the morning and who, when they do try to write in the afternoon, often end up having to practically rewrite everything all over again the following day. Gabriel Garcia Marquez recalls, "when I started writing full-time . . . I felt guilty that I was only working in the morning; so I tried to work in the afternoons, but I discovered that what I did in the afternoon had to be done over again the next morning. So I decided that I would just work from nine until two-thirty and not do anything else."[9]

Although the tendency to favor any given writing time slot over others is often seen as part of our natural makeup, it is important to distinguish biotemporal from strictly sociotemporal regularity[10] and note that such seemingly natural preferences often change quite dramatically to accommodate major changes in our *social* lifestyles, as when we get married, change jobs, or have children. When I was in graduate school, for example, I used to do most of my writing at night. Ever since my daughter started going to a daycare center, however, I have basically changed my regular work habits and come to "discover" that I am at my creative as well as productive best in the morning, which now, twenty years later, feels almost "natural" to me! As Toni Morrison has observed, "writing before dawn became a necessity—I had small children when I first began to write . . . [But many years later] I realized that I was clearer-headed, more confident and generally more intelligent in the morning. The habit of getting up early, which I had formed when the children were young, now became my choice."[11]

Ideals and Constraints

Having established the amount of time you plan to devote to your writing on a regular basis, broken it down into actual work sessions, as well as identified your best writing times, you can proceed now to design for yourself a regular writing schedule.

Paradoxical as it may sound, the best way to begin this process is actually by crossing off your regular daily as well as weekly schedule all the time slots during which you definitely cannot write on a regular basis and which should therefore not even be considered possible writing times! These include all the regular daily or weekly commitments and obligations that you regard as givens, such as the times you have to walk your dog, be at work, or take your son to his soccer practice. You should also cross off your schedule any other daily or weekly time slot during which you wish to be involved on a regular basis in activities other than writing—the night you play bridge or go to the movies, times of favorite television programs you like to watch, as well as the times you wish to reserve for reading and exercising, not to mention eating and sleeping.

Admittedly, the actual degrees of freedom you will have left at this point are considerably fewer than they would have been had you not taken this step. You may now realize that you actually have only twelve hours a week to devote to your writing this semester instead of the twenty-five hours you thought you would have, or that there is absolutely no way that you can realistically fit any of the four-hour morning sessions you want so much into your regular schedule. At the same time, having taken that preemptive step ought to

WRITERS ON BEST WRITING TIMES

I prefer the morning now, and just for two or three hours. In the beginning I used to work after midnight until dawn . . . [A]fter I got to Paris . . . I'd work in the morning, take a nap after lunch, get up and write again, sometimes write until midnight. In the last ten or fifteen years, I've found that it isn't necessary to work that much.

—Henry Miller[12]

I think the afternoon is a good time to work . . . It's a time when one's body is not at its sharpest, not at its most receptive—the body is quiescent, somnolent; but the brain can be quite sharp. I think also at the same time that the unconscious mind has a habit of asserting itself in the afternoon. The morning is the conscious time, but the afternoon is a time in which we should deal much more with the hinterland of the consciousness.

—Anthony Burgess[13]

I write at night. After the day is over, and supper is over, I begin, and work until about three or four A.M. . . . I've had to do that ever since I was young—I had to wait until the kids were asleep. And then I was working at various jobs during the day. I've always had to write at night. But now that I'm established I do it because I'm alone at night.

—James Baldwin[14]

I have a very rigorous work schedule. Every morning until two in the afternoon, I stay in my office. These hours are sacred to me. That doesn't mean I'm always writing; sometimes I'm revising or taking notes. But I remain systematically at work. There are, of course, the good days for creation and the bad ones. But I work every day.

—Mario Vargas Llosa[15]

Crossing off your weekly schedule the times you *cannot* write will allow you to define more realistically the times you *can*

	Monday	Tuesday	Wednesday	Thursday	Friday	Saturday	Sunday
7:00 A.M.							
8:00							
9:00							
10:00							
11:00							
12:00 P.M.							
1:00							
2:00							
3:00							
4:00							
5:00							
6:00							
7:00							
8:00							
9:00							
10:00							

give you the comforting knowledge that you have at least avoided a constant battle between your writing and your other high-priority involvements in life. And indeed, there is no reason why you should ever be in a position of having to pit your desire to write against your even greater desire to be a good parent or keep your job. Avoiding such a battle also gives you a much better chance to realize your goals as a writer than if you are unrealistically overambitious.

Avoiding a constant battle between your writing and your other involvements gives you a much better chance to realize your goals as a writer.

Needless to say, your final writing schedule will inevitably be a far cry from the ideal one you have considered earlier. Nevertheless, having considered a "dream" schedule becomes quite handy when you have at least some control over how to schedule the fifteen hours you need to put in every week as a freelance proofreader or your classes and office hours as a college professor. For example, if you see that you do your best writing in the morning, you should try to schedule those fifteen hours for afternoons or evenings rather than mornings. By the same token, if you find out that you are not a very productive writer on Mondays, you might want to try to schedule your classes and regular office hours for Mondays and Wednesdays rather than Tuesdays and Thursdays, which you may then reserve for your writing.

Having considered a "dream" schedule also gives you an

opportunity to create for yourself the best possible writing
conditions on those occasions when you can take off a couple
of days from work or when your children are staying with
friends for the weekend. On such occasions, when you get
to your desk, at least you know that you have indeed given
yourself the best chances to write well.

Quiet Times

Having established the amount of time you intend to devote
to your writing, broken it down into actual work sessions,
identified your best writing times, as well as crossed off your
calendar all the possible time slots during which you do *not*
plan to write on a regular basis, you can proceed now to
actually design your regular weekly writing schedule. And
the first thing you need to consider at this point is how to
minimize your chances of being interrupted so that you can
keep your "mental momentum" while you are writing.

Trying to protect your writing from possible interruptions
does not necessarily mean, of course, that you need to stay
literally "glued" for five or six straight hours to your key-
board. It does not preclude such mini-diversions as getting
up every once in a while to get a glass of water, do some
stretches, go to the bathroom, or even screen your incoming
electronic mail for particularly urgent messages. It does pre-
suppose, however, a certain continuity of concentration and
therefore precludes your getting too deeply involved in anything that might pull your attention in an altogether different
mental "direction" while you are trying to write.

Indeed, being able to do any creative mental work presupposes a temporary suspension of other obligations and

involvements that might compete with it for your immediate attention. It is extremely difficult, for example, to write a book when someone around you keeps talking to you or when your telephone or doorbell keeps ringing.

As one might expect, writers devise various strategies to help them protect their privacy when they are writing. Perhaps the most obvious one is trying to have their own private writing space. Indeed, Virginia Woolf regarded a separate office or study as the single most critical condition for being able to write.[16] Yet even that does not necessarily solve the problem of a telephone that keeps ringing. You need the freedom (as well as will) not to answer your phone while you are writing,[17] or at least to screen incoming calls with the help of a cooperative roommate, secretary, spouse, answering machine, or "Caller ID" kit. Some writers have gone even further. Maya Angelou, for example, keeps a hotel room in every town she has ever lived in: "I rent a hotel room for a few months, leave my home at six and try to be at work by 6:30 . . . I stay until 12:30 or 1:30 in the afternoon, and then I go home . . ."[18]

To fully appreciate the fundamental problem writers have faced ever since the invention of the telephone, arguably the greatest modern enemy of privacy, note that, as far as concentration is concerned, potential interruptions are very often just as disruptive as actual ones. The sheer knowledge that you *might* be interrupted any moment can make it extremely difficult to fully concentrate on what you are doing even when you are totally by yourself. That is why I usually try not to write whenever I am expecting an important telephone call. For the very same reason, I also never even try to do any serious writing in my office at the university, where somebody might knock on my door at any minute. In the past, whenever I tried to write under such conditions, I usually ended up having to rewrite everything I had written at that session all over again the following day.

Thus, when designing your regular weekly writing schedule, it is critical that you identify first the most "private" parts of your day and your week, when you are least likely to be interrupted,[19] and avoid as much as you can even trying to write at times when you expect that you might be. Such quiet times, however, you not only "find," but also actively *create* through effective scheduling. Thus, for example, many writers choose to write mainly in the morning, when "there is no one to disturb you" (Ernest Hemingway),[20] in a "quiet" time such as the afternoon (Anthony Burgess),[21] or at night, "when everybody has gone to bed and [one feels] completely at peace" (Tom Stoppard).[22] That, of course, is also why some parents, like the young Toni Morrison, try to write at dawn, before they hear the first cry of "Mommy,"[23] as well as why many others, like myself, opt to do most of their writing in the morning and early afternoon, when their children are at school and their immediate parental responsibilities are temporarily suspended.[24] While the quiet time slots may vary from one writer to another, our ultimate goal is basically the same—to be out of phase with our immediate social surroundings so as to minimize the risk of being interrupted when we are writing.

Keeping Your Momentum

Even beyond the level of the individual writing session, you need to be attentive to the continuous "flow" of your writing and keep it from being interrupted. When you are working on a large project (such as a thesis, a dissertation, or a book), which inevitably entails numerous sessions stretching over a long period of time, it is important to pay a lot of attention not only to when but also to *how often* you plan to write.

In order to ensure that you keep your "mental momentum" throughout the weeks, months, or even several years that you may have to work on the same project, try to minimize the number of times when you have to interrupt your writing for more than a day at a time. In other words, try to write as *frequently* as possible. The longer the time separating any two successive writing sessions on a given manuscript, the longer it will probably take you each session to recover your frame of mind from the last session. As one might expect, your writing may also be more choppy and less fluent at the level of entire sections or chapters.[25]

Being attentive to the continuous "flow" of your writing implies, of course, making a special effort to schedule your sessions back to back so as to allow yourself long stretches of relatively uninterrupted writing. Indeed, that is why many college professors often do most, if not all, of their writing during their summer vacations and sabbatical leaves, when they can afford to devote five, six, or sometimes even seven days every week to their writing. For the very same reason, try to write as frequently as possible and avoid being away from your manuscript for too long even during the more busy parts of the year. Thus, if you have the flexibility to do so (which is often the case when you are a college professor or a student), try to schedule all your regular commitments (classes, office hours, meetings) and obligations (returning telephone calls, answering letters, reviewing manuscripts, reading students' work in progress) either for the afternoon (if you like to write in the morning) or for the morning (if you prefer writing in the afternoon) but not for both on the same day. That will allow you to organize your writing in essentially continuous five-day stretches (or even longer ones if you are also willing and able to work on weekends) even during relatively busy periods.

Designing such a writing schedule may not always be possible, of course. Although I very much prefer to write regularly every weekday morning, during the school year I can only rarely write on Wednesdays, which is when my department holds its regular business meetings and colloquia. Indeed, for an entire eight-year period when I had a four-hour round-trip commute to work, I had to give up doing any writing on Mondays as well, as I preferred to squeeze all my commitments on campus into two full days rather than have to make five special trips there every week.

Furthermore, there is an inevitable tradeoff between the way you choose to space your writing sessions and the actual length of those sessions, and you basically need to decide whether length or frequency is more important to you, since one always comes at the expense of the other. After all, if the total amount of time you intend to spend on your writing remains constant, the closer together you schedule your sessions the shorter each of them is necessarily going to be. Choosing to schedule the ten hours you plan to devote to your writing every week so that you actually get to write every weekday morning rather than only on Mondays and Fridays, for example, will clearly help you avoid the considerable loss of mental momentum you are likely to suffer between sessions and save you the time you would probably need to spend at the beginning of each session trying to recapture the state of mind you were in three (on Mondays) or four (on Fridays) days earlier. It also means, however, that you will have to do all your writing in two-hour instead of five-hour stretches.

You can certainly train yourself, of course, to become more efficient and get a lot of work done even during such brief sessions, especially when you really have no other choice.[26] Indeed, that is how I managed over the course of two years to turn my doctoral dissertation into a book despite having a twelve-month, nine-to-five job. On the other hand, you may very well prefer having longer sessions that are somewhat closer to your ideal. You may find that you are willing to pay the inevitable price of losing some of your mental momentum between sessions in order to feel somewhat less "crowded" when you write.

A-Time and B-Time

In trying to design your regular weekly writing schedule, you have thus far considered only ideal or almost-ideal time slots while ignoring or even deliberately avoiding less-than-ideal ones. Those latter time slots, however, may nevertheless be used quite effectively for work that is directly related to your project yet requires less intense, focused concentration than your writing sessions. Thus, for example, you can make a lot of progress on somewhat "mechanical" tasks such as double-checking your footnotes even when you are waiting for an important telephone call or when your next-door neighbor is having a barbecue party and there is plenty of noise around you. By the same token, if in the middle of a regular four-hour writing session you suddenly realize that you are already tired and somewhat sluggish, there is no reason why you should not be able to use the remaining time to work on your bibliography, for which you certainly need not be "at your best."

There is also a lot of thinking you can do at such times. After all, there is no reason why you should burden your actual writing sessions with all the thinking you need to do on your project. And as the great Archimedes so vividly demonstrated when he took his famous bath twenty-three centuries ago, our best ideas do not always come to us only when we happen to be sitting at our desks. Although writing and thinking are not as distinct as we sometimes envision them, there is plenty of project-related thinking we can do between, rather than just during, our actual writing sessions.

Given all this, it is useful to learn to distinguish your "A-time," those somewhat sacred, "prime" time slots you choose to reserve for your writing and during which you obviously try to be at your very best, from mere "B-time" stretches, when you clearly do not have the proper conditions to write effectively yet may nevertheless be able to make considerable progress on various project-related tasks other than the actual writing itself.[27] During the years I had to commute to work, I learned to use the time I spent on the train (or waiting for it) to pre-edit sections of manuscripts I was going to revise the following day in my study. Over the years, I have likewise spent practically dozens of hours doing necessary project-related reading while waiting for various doctors, dentists, and barbers to see me.[28]

Such an effective use of B-time stretches is particularly significant in times of considerable pressure, when you need to do a lot of work in a relatively short period of time. And it is precisely the existence of such stretches (not to mention the even less ideal "C-time" stretches you might consider using for cleaning your kitchen or paying your bills) that allows you to make your A-time less interruptible.

You can also use such times to begin working on your next projects. Like four-burner stoves, our minds can quite easily handle multiple foci of attention simultaneously, though at somewhat different levels of intensity. Thus, even if at any given period you come to regard only one project as your main focus of intellectual attention, you can nevertheless still use your B-time to make some significant preliminary ("pre-writing") progress on other, future projects that are still simmering on your intellectual "back burners." As a result, by the time you are actually ready to start working on them in a more focused manner, you almost never have to begin from scratch!

CHAPTER 3

. . . .

A Mountain with Stairs

. . . .

Thus far we have examined the way in which we can use time to help us integrate our writing most effectively into the rest of our life. Let us turn now to examine how it can also help us organize the actual process of producing a particular manuscript. That entails, of course, approaching it not only circularly, as we do when we organize our writing in accordance with a regular weekly schedule, but also linearly.[1]

Divide and Conquer

One of the most formidable hurdles you will confront as a writer is the considerable amount of time separating the point when you actually start working on any given project from the point when you finally complete it. The problem is particularly serious, of course, when the project on which you happen to be working is not just a poem or a short essay but a much longer piece such as a thesis, a dissertation, or a book. The actual process of writing such a piece is extremely difficult psychologically, as it involves a rather distant and therefore somewhat elusive goal that can be reached only after a long and often trying time.

The sheer size of theses, dissertations, and books inevitably entails long periods of hard work that preclude immediate gratification. Unlike short stories or op-ed pieces, these are

Learn to think about your manuscript as a collection of smaller pieces.

obviously not projects that you can complete "in one gulp." And as you work on your project, you may have to grapple with the nagging question of whether you will manage to complete it. Like long-distance runners, cross-country bikers, and mountain climbers, writers traverse a long road paved with serious doubts, wondering whether they will ever be able to reach their final goal. Their actual "distance" from this goal, which, like the top of a high mountain that lies hidden behind a seemingly impenetrable screen of clouds, they can only vaguely envision, understandably generates a paralyzing amount of anxiety. Intimidated by the enormity of the task that lies ahead of them, many writers indeed break down somewhere along that ominous road and never complete their projects.

Much of this problem could be avoided if the prospect of completing a thesis, a book, or a dissertation were not so intimidating. Fortunately enough, that can be arranged easily through some careful planning. The solution lies in learning to think about your manuscript not only as one single piece but also as a collection of a number of smaller, and therefore more manageable, pieces. That allows you to essentially transform what may otherwise seem like a rather intimidating task into a series of relatively nonintimidating mini-tasks. After all, the same twenty-six-mile course seems much less fearsome to marathon runners once they manage to break it down in their heads into twenty-six separate one-mile segments, for the same reason that a large chunk of meat seems much less overwhelming to a child once it is cut into several bite-sized pieces.

In other words, you can quite easily manage the most formidable tasks if you only learn to break them down in your head into a number of less ambitious and thus also less intimidating mini-tasks, the completion of each of which is well within your reach. You must therefore stop regarding the completion of the entire thesis, book, or dissertation you are writing as your only goal and concentrate instead on completing each of the various segments into which you have broken it down, *one at a time.* Having to deal at any given time with only one small and therefore relatively nonintimidating segment will inevitably free you from the tremendous psychological pressure of having to constantly grapple with your entire manuscript as a whole. Thus, if you have difficulties with the second section of the third chapter, you will not feel as compelled to give up on your entire book or dissertation.

Setting for yourself several mini-goals along the road to your ultimate goal basically allows you to proceed incrementally by taking only one step at a time. Since climbing each of those mental stairs is relatively simple, instead of a single seemingly unaccomplishable task you will actually be dealing with a series of relatively unproblematic mini-tasks that you clearly *can* manage.

Breaking down a single monumental task into a number of smaller and thus considerably less intimidating mini-tasks also enhances your sense of accomplishment. Instead of a single, delayed feeling of accomplishment you may get to experience only once every several months or even years upon completing an entire manuscript, you can have numerous such experiences while you are writing it. After all, if you break down your dissertation or book into seven chapters, each of which is further divided into three sections, and proceed to write four drafts of each, you may actually have eighty-four different opportunities to enjoy the sense of accomplishment associated with the experience of completing *anything*. Such an experience will inevitably boost your confidence and further prevent you from breaking down at some point along the way and abandoning it altogether.

The Outline

The simplest way to mentally package a manuscript in smaller, psychologically more manageable ("chewable") chunks is to break it down into chapters and each chapter further down into sections, and then deal with each of those inevitably less intimidating segments separately, one at a time. Thus, when you are working on the second section of the fourth chapter of your dissertation, for example, you can focus your entire psychological (as well as intellectual) attention on that section alone while putting all the rest of the manuscript temporarily on hold on some mental "back burner."

In order to effectively segment your manuscript, however, you need to have a general outline, a skeletal blueprint that somehow encapsulates its basic structure. To develop such an outline, you need to break down your entire project into the actual steps that would be necessary to complete it and arrange them systematically in an itinerary-like sequence. Like building contractors, military strategists, and travel agents, writers need to devote a lot of attention to this extremely critical phase of their projects. Even after finishing my doctoral dissertation, I still spent practically two months trying to reorganize its contents in accordance with a somewhat modified outline before I began to rewrite it as a book.

Having an outline helps you think linearly, which is indispensable when you are working on a long manuscript. Unless you carefully plan your writing in a linear fashion, you may never be able to develop a clear sense of where you are in your manuscript and of the general direction in which you are basically going, so that every time you sit down to write you may end up having to spend a lot of time re-reading what you have already written and trying to recall where exactly you wanted to go the last time you were writing. People who do not use an outline when they write usually find themselves going in circles, which makes it quite difficult for them to produce a single coherent manuscript rather than a mere collection of disjointed patches.

To ensure that the actual building blocks of your outline may indeed serve as mental stairs that you can comfortably "climb," you clearly need to make them small enough. When designing the general outline of your manuscript, you may discover that even sections within chapters are sometimes too large to "chew" and may therefore need to be further broken down into subsections or even paragraphs (even if in your final draft you choose not to present these as distinct units with separate titles in the actual text).

Breaking anything down into discrete mental segments, however, always entails the danger of somehow forgetting that these segments are products of our own minds.[2] Thus, when you break down a manuscript into chapters and sections within chapters, you need to recognize their essentially arbitrary nature and remember that they can still be further rearranged (as well as recombined) if you so wish. In other words, rather than regard your outline as an inevitable structure with which you are basically stuck forever, you should realize that you can actually change it many times while you are working on your manuscript.

Thus, at any given point during the course of writing your thesis, dissertation, or book you need to regard its general outline as no more than a provisional, tentative arrangement. Having originally planned to organize your ideas in a particular manner should not preclude the possibility of reorganizing them later in some other manner as many times as you practically wish. All it may require is a certain degree of mental flexibility.[3]

Consider, for example, my own book *The Fine Line.* Before I actually began writing it, I had only five general categories for organizing in my mind what I thought it would include:

1. Boundaries in Space and Time
2. Boundaries between Categories
3. Frames
4. Cognitive Distance and Affinity
5. Cognitive Purity and Pollution

By the time I started working on my first draft, however, I already had the following rough outline to guide me:

Introduction
1. Waves and Particles
    Boundaries in Space
    Boundaries in Time
    Frames and "Realities"
    Boundaries of Categories
2. The Eye of the Beholder
    Social Conventions and Norms
    Culture and Variability
    Boundary Disputes
    Reification
3. Drawing the Line
    Metamessages
    Rites of Passage
    Cognitive Order and Anomie
4. Purity and Rigidity
    Separation, Segregation, and Exclusivity
    Anomalies and Ambiguity
    Society and Rigidity
5. Flexibility and Fluidity
6. Creativity and Order

Three of my initial five "proto-chapters" (the first, second, and third) had already become mere sections within the new first chapter, "Waves and Particles." Furthermore, four of the six new chapters (the second, third, fifth, and sixth) had not even been contemplated initially!

This new outline, however, changed again quite dramatically by the time I completed the first full draft of my manuscript and began working on the second:

Introduction
1. Particles and Partitions
    Spatial Particles
    The Ego
    Quasi-Spatial Particles
    Temporal Particles
    Frames
    Mental Distance and Proximity
    Difference and Similarity
2. The Rigid Mind
    Segregation and Exclusion
    Ego Boundaries
    Us and Them
    Loci of Rigidity
    Separation and Passage
3. The Social Eye of the Beholder
    The Politics of Classification
    The Social Glasses
    The Fuzzy and the Gray
4. A World with No Lines
    The Ocean
    Fantasy, Ritual, and Play
    Fluidity in Art and Design
    Fluidity in Ideology
    Fluidity and Culture

Perhaps most noticeably, the chapters "Drawing the Line" and "Creativity and Order" disappeared as distinct chapters, although the former's first two sections were essentially recombined to form the new section "Separation and Passage" (in the same way that the old sections "Social Conventions and Norms" and "Culture and Variability" were essentially recombined to form the new section "The Social Glasses"). Furthermore, the old fourth chapter became the new second chapter, whereas the old second chapter became the new third chapter. Some brand new sections ("The Ego," "Quasi-Spatial Particles," "Ego Boundaries," "Us and Them") were added, some old ones ("Cognitive Order and Anomie," "Anomalies and Ambiguity") were abandoned, and the old proto-chapter "Cognitive Distance and Affinity" from the initial outline was essentially "resurrected" as a new section ("Mental Distance and Proximity") in the first chapter. The chapter "Flexibility and Fluidity" (renamed "A World with No Lines") was likewise broken down into five separate sections.

Yet even this new outline was somewhat transformed by the time I completed the second draft of my manuscript and began working on the third:

Introduction
1. Islands of Meaning
    Chunks of Space
    Blocks of Time
    Frames
    Chunks of Identity
    Mental Fields
    Ritual Transitions
2. The Great Divide
    Mental Gaps

    Mental Quantum Leaps
    Mental Images and Social Reality
3. The Rigid Mind
    Purity and Order
    Self and Environment
    Social Segregation
    The Psychological Roots of Rigidity
    Rigid Social Environments
4. The Social Lens
    Culture and Classification
    The Color Gray
    The Social Construction of Discontinuity
5. The Fuzzy Mind
    The Ocean
    Letting Go
    Opening Up
    Ritual Fluidity
    Playful Promiscuity
    Comic Transgression
    Fluidity in Art
    The Ethics of Fluidity
    Fluidity and Modernity
6. The Flexible Mind
    Transgression and Creativity
    Boundaries and Order
    Mental Plasticity

This new outline (which survived the third and fourth drafts of my manuscript and thus turned out to be the book's table of contents) included two new chapters: the old section "Mental Distance and Proximity" was reconstituted as the new second chapter, "The Great Divide," whereas the old last proto-chapter ("Creativity and Order") from the initial outline, which I had essentially abandoned in the first draft, was resurrected (although with an altogether new last section, "Mental Plasticity"). Some brand new sections ("Letting Go," "Opening Up," "Comic Transgression") were likewise added, the old section "Loci of Rigidity" was further broken down into two new ones ("The Psychological Roots of Rigidity" and "Rigid Social Environments"), and the last section of the second chapter (renamed "Ritual Transitions") was essentially moved back to the first.

To avoid going "in circles," however, you should make such major structural changes in your manuscript only *between* drafts, when you are not actually writing. Within each draft, it is better to stick to the same outline even when you realize that it is just a provisional blueprint that may still change many times later on. Although it is obviously not carved in stone, having even a tentative structure is always preferable to having no structure at all.[4]

Furthermore, if you constantly keep "reshuffling" your ideas, you will never get to complete writing anything! It may be helpful to remind yourself, in this regard, that even great classics such as Plato's *Republic,* Deuteronomy, and the *Tao Te Ching* were ultimately organized in only one of the numerous possible ways in which they could have been.

Drafts and Revisions

Breaking down a thesis, dissertation, or book into chapters and sections within chapters certainly helps relieve some of the tremendous psychological pressure normally generated by having to produce a manuscript of such intimidating magnitude. It is usually also complemented, however, by the practice of writing it in several drafts.

At first glance, such a paradoxical solution may actually seem even more intimidating than the problem it is designed to remedy. Having to write an entire dissertation or book several times certainly sounds much more anxiety-provoking than having to do it only once. Yet it is precisely the fact that you can actually write it more than just once that helps relieve much of the pressure as well as reduce much of the anxiety normally involved in having to write it at all. After all, with the exception of the very final draft (which, after having gone through several earlier drafts, often involves little more than just adding some final touches), within each draft you can "let go" and write in a much more relaxed manner knowing that it is not your last chance and that you have at least one more opportunity to improve later on what you are currently writing.

Writing a thesis or a dissertation in several drafts instead of just one entails some other, extra-psychological benefits as well. When I was in college, I used to take great pride in the fact that I would hand in virtually unrevised term papers, and basically regarded "having to" write more than one draft as an intellectual problem I fortunately did not have. I have since learned the value of revision. Contrary to the common romantic image of the act of creating (and of the creator as a "genius"), very few great literary or scholarly pieces are actually produced in one draft.

One of the most common misconceptions inexperienced writers have of writing is that it is simply a mechanical process of reproducing already-formed ideas on paper. Nothing could be farther from the truth. In reality, writing is virtually inseparable from the process of developing our ideas. In other words, much of our thinking actually takes place *while* we are writing!

I thus recommend writing a thesis, dissertation, or book in several drafts not only for writers who simply cannot manage to do it in only one draft, but for *all* writers. Although you may very well end up producing acceptable, and sometimes even good, manuscripts in only one draft, you may never get to find out how much deeper, more sophisticated, and more polished those pieces might have been had you revised that first draft two or three times. As anyone who has

· ·

WRITERS ON REVISING

Every book is worked over several times. I like to compare my method with that of painters . . . proceeding, as it were, from layer to layer. The first draft is quite crude, far from being perfect, by no means finished . . . After that I rewrite it as many times—applying as many "layers" as I feel to be necessary.

—Alberto Moravia[5]

First drafts are for learning what your [book] is about. Revision is working with that knowledge to enlarge and enhance an idea, to re-form it. D. H. Lawrence, for instance, did seven or eight drafts of *The Rainbow* . . . Revision is one of the true pleasures of writing.

—Bernard Malamud[6]

· ·

ever painted a room knows, although we eventually get to see only the last coat that has been applied to a wall, it is actually the extra coat underneath it that usually gives the final product its somewhat richer texture.

The actual number of drafts one needs to write inevitably varies from writer to writer, since it depends on highly idiosyncratic personal characteristics such as temperament and stamina. In general, however, you should try to identify an optimal number that would not be too low, so as to allow yourself to take off some of the psychological pressure from each particular draft, yet at the same time also not too high, so as to avoid the risk of burnout that usually affects anyone who spends too much time on any given project. I personally prefer to write everything in four drafts, having found out over the years that only two or three drafts do not allow me to write in a relaxed enough manner yet that five are clearly one too many for my patience.[7]

How many drafts you need, of course, also depends on what you consider a "draft." For some writers, for example, it clearly entails little more than some light editing. For others, it involves some major revising. For me it entails rewriting my entire manuscript from start to finish.

There is also the question whether you write by hand, on a typewriter, or on a computer. And although in every one of those three modes of writing each "draft" may actually consist of several "pre-drafts" at the level of each paragraph or group of paragraphs, this is particularly true when you are writing on a computer, which allows you to keep editing and revising your manuscript indefinitely before actually committing yourself to any tangible, "hard" copy. Thus, although I technically write a book in four drafts, various sentences within

it may have been rewritten ten or fifteen different times. A
"draft" for me, then, involves making a decision at a certain
point to print out the version with which I am willing to live
at least until the next draft, and move on to the next segment
of my manuscript.

Whether in each draft you do only some minor editing or
actually rewrite entire sections, I strongly suggest that you
write your thesis, dissertation, or book several times *from
start to finish* rather than try to bring each segment of your
manuscript to completion and only then move on to the next
one. This will help reduce the chances that you would somehow break down in mid-course and abandon your entire project altogether, which is what often happens to students who,
in a shortsighted effort to relieve their more immediate anx-
ieties, choose to bring each chapter of their dissertation to a
point where it is approved by their advisor before moving on
to the next one.

To better understand my strongly preferred choice between
those two contrasting strategies, consider the case of a college
professor I once met who, at the end of a highly productive
sabbatical year abroad during which he managed to write
more than three quarters of a book manuscript, found himself
just two chapters short of fully completing it. Unfortunately,
he had not even started writing those two chapters and, being
well aware of the rather stringent time constraints he would
soon have to face back home, sadly accepted the fact that it
would probably take him another few years before he would
be able to find the time to start working on them. His entire
book, in other words, had to wait several more years before
he could finish it.

Such a problem would not have arisen in the first place

had he not put himself in the extremely difficult position of having to produce those two remaining chapters out of nothing. After all, it is always much easier to simply revise something than to create it from scratch, and if you write your dissertation or book several times from start to finish you will inevitably reach much sooner a certain point of no return when you already have an entire manuscript under your belt! Though it obviously still requires a lot of work, even at that relatively early point in your project you no longer have to face the "great void"[8] typically associated with having to create something from scratch, since the end of the tunnel is already in sight.

In other words, having at least some form of a full-length manuscript in hand so early in the process of writing it allows you to experience much sooner a goal that does not require years of waiting. After all, once you complete your first draft, you know that your book or thesis is there, a mental lump of clay that you can start molding.[9] As Mario Vargas Llosa puts it, "the first version is written in a real state of anxiety. Then once I've finished that draft . . . everything changes. *I know then that the story is there,* buried in what I call my 'magma.' It's absolute chaos but the novel is in there, lost in a mass of dead elements, superfluous scenes that will disappear . . . It's very chaotic and makes sense only to me. But the story is born under there."[10]

Aside from such a tremendous psychological boost, writing your thesis, dissertation, or book several times from start to finish also entails considerable intellectual benefits. First, it helps you to maintain a more uniform authorial voice as well as a more even "tone" throughout your manuscript, thereby making it somewhat easier for you to produce a relatively seamless single piece rather than a mere collection of essentially disjointed fragments. "Tying in" what you write in Chapter 8 with what you wrote only a couple of months earlier in Chapter 5 is a lot simpler than it would have been had you completed Chapter 5 almost a year earlier, before you even began working on Chapters 6 and 7.

Furthermore, writing your manuscript several times from start to finish clearly helps you to achieve greater textual consistency as well as to avoid redundancy not only in each particular chapter but also in your manuscript as a whole. Indeed, that is why it would also be somewhat pointless now to expect your editor to give you any definitive feedback on the third chapter of your book when she is still not absolutely sure what you will be writing next year when you finally start working on the sixth and seventh chapters. By the same token, it would also be much less useful for you to have the second and third chapters of your dissertation read by your advisor several months apart from each other, which is inevitably what happens when you work on each single chapter separately and try to get it approved before moving on to the next one.

By producing several drafts from start to finish, you will also maximize the quality of what you produce. If you distribute your creative "highs" and "lows" across drafts that are written months or even years apart, you can achieve the kind of smooth, high-quality consistency one usually tries to achieve when spreading butter or jelly on a slice of bread. Thus, even if during the entire period that you are working on the first draft of a particular section in your manuscript you happen to feel somewhat uninspired (which is not that uncommon when you are writing according to a regular schedule rather than only by inspiration), at least you know that you will still have several other opportunities to revisit that section, and that it is highly unlikely that you would end up feeling just as uninspired at *all* of them as well.

Yet the most important intellectual benefit of writing your thesis, book, or dissertation several times from start to finish is the fact that, although the "net" amount of time you end up spending on any specific segment of your manuscript is roughly the same as when you try to bring each chapter or section to completion before moving on to the next one, the actual "gross" amount of time involved in writing it is considerably greater.[11] Since the entire manuscript is being practically rewritten each draft, more time inevitably separates the first and final versions of any particular section in it!

Extending the "gross" amount of time you get to spend on any given section of your book or dissertation offers you a greater opportunity to generate some new ideas (especially ones that may require a long "incubation" period) and perhaps even approach that section from a somewhat different perspective on your next draft. It also ensures a higher degree of intellectual "ripeness" to every single segment of your manuscript. Otherwise, the last chapters to be written often reflect the highest peak you manage to reach in terms of developing your ideas, while the first ones are much less refined—a common problem with completing the first chapter of your dissertation one or two years before the last chapter. After all, the fact that you would never produce a final version of any chapter before you even begin working on another inevitably implies that, paradoxical as it may sound, your work on later chapters of your manuscript can still affect what you will be writing in earlier ones! You can still generate new ideas for (the third draft of) the fourth chapter while already working on (the second draft of) the seventh. None of this is possible when you try to bring each chapter of your book or dissertation to completion before moving on to the next one.

Indeed, the whole idea of working with a flexible, "evolving" outline that may keep changing from time to time only makes sense if you rewrite your entire manuscript from start to finish each draft. Otherwise, would you even consider the possibility of perhaps weaving the third chapter of your dissertation into the sixth chapter, for example, when it has already been completed and essentially approved by your advisor more than a year ago?

The only major exception to all this involves the introduction. It is very difficult to write the opening chapter of a dissertation or a book unless you are absolutely sure of its contents and your general conclusion, which very often is not the case. It is quite all right, therefore, to write the introduction only after having written all the rest of your manuscript first, which basically means skipping it altogether in the first draft. I often start working on my introduction only in the second draft, after having already been through the entire manuscript once and thus developing at least a basic "feel" for the general direction in which it is going.

Of course, if you are already used to trying to bring chapters or sections within chapters to completion before moving on to the next ones, learning to write a draft of an entire manuscript from start to finish may not be that easy. As you forgo the luxury of enjoying early gratification in the form of fully-completed segments, you may experience some anxiety about the prospect of having to write several drafts of an entire dissertation or book before you ever get to see *any* segment fully completed. And yet, whereas people who complete segments of manuscripts very often do not get to complete those manuscripts, you can rest assured that once you have completed a first full draft of your manuscript you will almost never fail to get to the top of the mountain and complete your project in its entirety.

. . . .

The Project Timetable

. . . .

Now that you have planned *how* to complete your manuscript, you can proceed to begin the process of designing an actual timetable for your project. Doing that, however, presupposes thinking about time not only in structural terms of "before" and "after" but also in calendrical terms of weeks, months, and actual deadlines. Having broken down your manuscript into chapters and sections within chapters and considered the psychological as well as intellectual benefits of writing it several times from start to finish, you can now start calculating how much time you will need to spend on each chapter and whether you can promise to show your advisor or editor a full draft of your thesis, dissertation, or book by next July.

Estimating Length

The first step in designing an effective timetable for your project involves making a comprehensive list of the various "stairs" leading to the top of the mental mountain representing your thesis, dissertation, or book and estimating the approximate "height" of each stair. In other words, you first need to assign each of the constituent segments of your manuscript an estimated length.

The most convenient way to estimate the lengths of the various segments of your manuscript is in terms of number of pages (assuming, of course, the establishment of some personal *standard* notion of "a page" in terms of paper size, margins, line spacing, as well as font size). That means learning to think about chapters and sections within chapters as "thirty-page" or "twelve-page" blocks of text.

Estimating the lengths of chapters and sections within chapters is particularly hard when you are designing the timetable for the first draft of your manuscript, since, having to essentially write it from scratch, there is still very little you can go by. Yet even at that early stage you can already make at least some rough projections, especially if you have a relatively detailed outline of your manuscript. For example, by simply asking yourself progressively whether you can even imagine it being, say, (a) fifty, (b) thirty, (c) twenty, or (d) ten pages long, you can already project quite confidently that it is highly unlikely that a particular section of the first draft of your thesis, dissertation, or book would end up being more than seven or eight pages long.

On such occasions, however, I strongly suggest that you designate that section on your project timetable as a ten-page rather than a seven- or eight-page "stair." By deliberately *overestimating* the length of each segment of your manuscript, you certainly reduce the chances that you will fail to accomplish later the goals you have set for yourself. After all, if you keep overestimating the size of your chapters (as well as sections within chapters), you are much more likely to experience later the pleasant "surprise" of actually beating the deadlines you project for completing them! Therefore, if you expect a particular section of your dissertation to be four or

$\mathcal{D}$eliberately overestimate the length of each segment of your manuscript to reduce the chance of failing to reach your goals.

five pages long, base your projection on six or seven pages instead. In other words, try to avoid the common temptation to underestimate the size of your project, or else you may experience later the inevitable disappointment and sense of failure associated with not having managed to accomplish the goals you have set for yourself.

Overestimating the length of your manuscript will save you a lot of anxiety and pressure later on, as you begin to approach the deadline you have set for completing it. It also helps you build into your timetable a kind of "shock absorber" that becomes quite handy whenever your projected plans are unexpectedly interrupted, which is bound to happen at some point. Building into every single constituent segment of your thesis, book, or dissertation a "safety cushion" of a few extra pages beyond your estimate will help your timetable survive even extremely "slow" periods when you are sick, unexpectedly overburdened with other commitments, or simply "behind."

Once you have completed your first draft, of course, estimating the length of any given segment of your manuscript
becomes a much simpler task, since you have an earlier draft
to go by. Thus, for example, in order to estimate the length
of the third draft of the second section of the fourth chapter
of your dissertation, you need to simply add to the length of
the already-completed *second* draft of that section a certain
(again, preferably slightly overestimated) number of pages
based on the amount of new ideas you have generated and
new data you have collected since having completed it. On
the basis of that you can estimate that what is now a six-page
segment, for example, will probably expand into nine pages
(or shrink into four pages if you are planning to do a lot of
cutting) in your next draft.

Based on such projections, you can now transform your
chapter-and-section outline into an actual timetable by adding rough estimates of the lengths of the various constituent
segments of the next draft of your manuscript.

There is no reason, of course, to assume or even expect
that the length of any given segment of your thesis, book, or
dissertation will remain exactly the same as you keep moving
from one draft of your manuscript to the next one. Indeed,
given the nature of the process of revising, it will probably
change several times during the course of writing it. A section
that you initially envision being twelve pages long, for example, may thus end up being fourteen pages long once you
start working on your second draft yet only eight by the time
you get to the fourth. That means, of course, that you must
keep revising your timetable whenever you complete a full
draft of your manuscript and are ready to move on to the
next one.

Estimating the length of a manuscript

Pacing Yourself

The next necessary step in the process of designing an effective timetable for your project is "translating" the terms in which you estimate the length of your manuscript from the language of text (number of pages) to the language of time. Doing that, however, requires adding yet another temporal dimension beyond just sequence to your outline.

This still-missing dimension, of course, is the pace of your projected "movement" through your manuscript, the estimated *speed* at which you actually plan to climb each of the various stairs leading to the top of the mental mountain representing it. And in the same way that seasoned long-distance runners try to project how long it will take them to complete a marathon course by carefully setting the pace at which they intend to cover each of its twenty-six constituent miles, you can project approximately how long it will take you to complete your thesis, dissertation, or book by carefully setting the pace at which you plan to be writing each of its chapters.

Pacing yourself presupposes some regular "counting cycle"[1] against which you can actually measure the speed of activities such as running or writing. You can thus set for yourself a regular quota of a certain number of words to be generated every hour, for example, or a certain number of chapters to be completed every year.

It would probably be in your best interest to avoid pacing yourself in accordance with cycles that are somewhat too long when you write, since they are obviously not sensitive enough for your purposes and would therefore not allow you to get constant feedback on how you are moving along. For the same reason that marathon runners usually pace themselves in terms of a certain number of minutes per mile rather than per ten miles, it does not make sense for you to pace your writing by the year or even by the month. You do not want to have to wait that long every time you wish to monitor your progress.

At the same time, however, it is also important to avoid pacing yourself in accordance with cycles that are somewhat too short when you write, since they are obviously much *too* sensitive for your purposes and may therefore lead you to deviate from your set pace much too often. Just as marathon runners usually pace themselves in terms of a certain number of minutes per mile rather than a certain number of seconds per twenty-five yards, it makes absolutely no sense for you to pace yourself by the minute or even by the hour when you write because of the number of times you will almost inevitably end up falling behind your set pace.

Given all that, I strongly recommend that when you work on a project of such magnitude as a thesis, dissertation, or book, you pace yourself in terms of a certain number of pages to be completed per day. Add a new "Pace" column to your project timetable, as I have done in the boxed example.

There are several important factors you need to consider when setting the pace at which you plan to be writing your thesis, dissertation, or book. Indeed, you should expect some significant variations in pace among different manuscripts you produce, among different segments of any given manuscript, as well as among different drafts of any given segment.

Writers often work on different manuscripts at different speeds. Having managed to maintain a steady pace of seven pages a day while he was working on *The Naked and the Dead*, for example, Norman Mailer could produce only three pages

Estimating the pace of writing a manuscript

Section	Length (pages)	Pace (pages per day)
Introduction	5	1
1. Islands of Meaning		
Chunks of Space	2	1.5
Blocks of Time	2	1.5
Frames	4	2
Chunks of Identity	2	2
Mental Fields	5	1.5
Ritual Transitions	5	2
2. The Great Divide		
Mental Gaps	4	1.5
Mental Quantum Leaps	5	1.5
Mental Images and Social Reality	7	1
3. The Rigid Mind		
Purity and Order	5	2.5
Self and Environment	3	2
Social Segregation	11	2
The Psychological Roots of Rigidity	6	1.5
Rigid Social Environments	13	2.5
4. The Social Lens		
Culture and Classification	12	2
The Color Gray	6	1.5
The Social Construction of Discontinuity	8	1.5
5. The Fuzzy Mind		
The Ocean	7	1.5
Letting Go	2	1.5
Opening Up	2	1.5
Ritual Fluidity	2	2
Playful Promiscuity	4	2
Comic Transgression	4	2
Fluidity in Art	5	2
The Ethics of Fluidity	3	2.5
Fluidity and Modernity	12	2
6. The Flexible Mind		
Transgression and Creativity	3	1.5
Boundaries and Order	3	1
Mental Plasticity	5	1

a day when he was writing *Barbary Shore*.[2] For one thing, one usually works much more slowly on projects that are somewhat more ambitious. It took me six years to complete *The Fine Line* yet only two to write *The Seven-Day Circle,* which is almost exactly the same length. Pressure, too, plays an important role. One usually works much faster on manuscripts one needs to complete right before coming up for tenure.

There is a somewhat smaller-scale version of such variations *within* any given manuscript, as different segments often require different paces of progress. Thus you will need to proceed much more slowly on sections that are more technically complex and therefore require a somewhat greater effort on your part to present your argument or findings in a way that would be accessible to your readers. Although it ended up being less than five pages long, it took me a couple of weeks, for example, to produce each draft of the section on the traditional Mexican calendar in *The Seven-Day Circle* simply because the material I presented in it was so technically complex. Chapters as well as sections within chapters that involve more complex arguments likewise require a much slower pace than ones that are somewhat less intellectually demanding.

Another important factor that may affect how fast you can write any given segment of your manuscript is the amount of preliminary work you may have completed already before you even begin writing it. Thus, when I started working on *Hidden Rhythms* or *Social Mindscapes,* for example, I had a good reason to expect a somewhat easier time (and therefore also project a somewhat faster pace for) writing chapters that were to be based on some earlier work I had done, than chapters that I would basically be writing from scratch.

By the same token, except when you are still working on your first draft, you also need to take into consideration the amount of new material (ideas as well as data) you have generated for any given segment of your manuscript since the previous draft. Thus, when I was writing *The Fine Line,* for example, the number of new ideas I kept generating for sections like "Mental Gaps," "The Psychological Roots of Rigidity," and "Mental Plasticity" was so great that I decided to set for those sections a pace of a page and a half or even just a page a day. Sections like "Rigid Social Environments" and "The Ethics of Fluidity," on the other hand, seemed to require much less work each new draft and could therefore be written at a much faster pace of two and a half pages a day.

There are similar variations in pace among the various *drafts* of any given manuscript, as many writers tend to work on different drafts at somewhat different speeds. For some, first drafts are particularly stressful and therefore also tend to be written much more slowly than other drafts.[3] For others, it is precisely the other way around. I personally like to set a somewhat faster pace for my first draft, so as to get myself going,[4] as well as for my fourth and final draft, which by the time I get to it is already quite polished and usually requires only some minor touch-ups, and work more slowly on my second and third drafts, which often involve full-scale revisions of my entire manuscript.

Whatever your personal preference, you will probably keep making changes in the "Pace" column of your project timetable as you keep moving from one draft to the next. Such periodic updating of your timetable may indeed be necessary until your entire manuscript is fully completed.

Regardless of how fast you actually write, I strongly suggest that you always set a certain "speed limit" on how fast you *plan* to be moving along so as to keep your excess ambition in check. For the same reason that you need to overestimate the length of your manuscript, you should also deliberately underestimate the pace at which you will be writing it.[5] In other words, always try to set for yourself a pace that is somewhat slower than what you expect to achieve.

There is nothing inherently wrong, of course, with setting a fast pace of progress if you are actually going to be able to sustain it. Doing that, however, usually involves a lot of pressure that takes much of the fun out of your writing. Hence the tremendous advantage of planning to write at a pace that is not only manageable but also feels comfortable to you. Furthermore, being overly ambitious makes it almost inevitable that you will experience some disappointment later. Our sense of accomplishment is a function of not only how well we actually do but also what our initial expectations were, and the absence of some clear checks on your ambition is bound to leave you feeling somewhat unfulfilled. Indeed, you are much more likely to achieve satisfaction by wanting less than by having more.[6] The most effective way for you to maximize your sense of accomplishment and minimize your experience of disappointment and sense of failure, therefore, is to establish from the very start a somewhat lower level of expectations and only set for yourself goals that are definitely within your reach. After all, while writing a first draft of a chapter of your dissertation in twelve days may be satisfying, it is not nearly as satisfying as writing it in twelve days after having originally planned to write it in twenty!

This means, of course, that you need to be somewhat less "greedy" and grandiose when designing your project time-table and to avoid setting goals that you may not be able to

stablish a somewhat lower level of expecta-tions—only set for yourself goals that are definitely within your reach.

meet (such as making unrealistic plans for the summer or your coming sabbatical leave). Setting a sustainable pace will certainly help increase your chances of meeting your dead-lines and avoiding disappointment and failure later on.

Given all this, I usually make a conscious effort not to succumb to the common temptation to overreach, and only rarely commit myself in my project timetables to producing more than two or two and a half double-spaced pages per work session. In fact, I normally plan to write only a page and a half a day. Interestingly enough, very few writers actu-ally write as fast as we sometimes think they do. E. L. Doctorow once admitted, "If I do one page I'm very happy; that's my day's work. If I do two, that's extraordinary."[7] Sim-ilarly, to Kingsley Amis, "two pages a day is good. Three pages is splendid."[8] Indeed, even the extremely prolific Graham Greene used to write only two pages a day.[9] And as he planned the writing of *East of Eden,* John Steinbeck likewise noted in his diary: "But I am not going to speed up. I just can't do it and keep with it for that length of time. Two of these pages is just about right for the pace of this book . . . *Slow and easy does it*."[10]

It is important to recognize that moving along so slowly should not prevent one from becoming a prolific writer (it certainly has not stopped me from completing seven books over the past twenty-one years) because, unlike grocery shopping or housecleaning, writing is cumulative, and even days on which we actually end up writing only a page and a half ultimately add up. Like piggy-bank savers whose nickels and pennies are eventually "transformed" into actual dollars, even writers who proceed extremely slowly nevertheless end up producing full-length manuscripts. Indeed, there are few experiences as exhilarating as watching a seemingly meager daily harvest of only a page and a half gradually blossoming into a full-fledged thesis, dissertation, or book.

As it very often does, the secret, of course, lies in perseverance. You may thus produce only a page and a half a day yet still end up with a complete dissertation as long as, like Aesop's proverbial tortoise, you are continually persistent, slow yet steady. As the extremely prolific Philip Roth sums up this remarkably mundane process: "I work . . . just about every day. If I sit there like that for two or three years, at the end I have a book."[11]

Deadlines

By setting the pace at which you plan to be working on the various constituent segments of your manuscript, you implicitly set the actual amount of time you think it will take you to complete writing them. By simply dividing the estimated

length (in terms of number of pages) of each of those segments by the pace (in terms of number of pages per day) at
which you intend to work on it, you can basically project the
approximate amount of time (in terms of number of working
days) it will take you to actually write it. Add a new column,
labeled "Time," to your project timetable.

By now you should have a pretty good idea of the approximate amount of time it is going to take you to climb each of
the various stairs leading to the top of the mental mountain
representing your thesis, dissertation, or book. Such "time,"
however, is quite different from the time designated on your
calendar.

As evident from the way we usually reckon time in bas-
ketball, chess, and ice hockey, it is quite possible to dissociate
measured ("net") time from actual passing ("gross") time,[12]
and thus far you have projected your progress strictly in
terms of the former. Yet while "fourteen days" of writing
indeed mean two weeks during a quiet winter break when
you can actually write seven days a week, they may also
stretch over an entire semester during the school year, when
you only get to write on Fridays.

You are entering now the final stage of the process of
designing your project timetable, when you need to convert
the "net" number of working days currently listed in the right
column of your timetable into actual deadlines for the completion of each of the various constituent segments of your
manuscript. In other words, it is time to lay your project
timetable over a conventional calendar.[13]

First, identify the actual days on which you plan to do your
writing and block them off on your calendar. Ironically, as
we have seen earlier, the best way to begin doing that is by

Estimating how long it will take to write a manuscript

Section	Length (pages)	Pace (pages per day)	Time (days)
Introduction	5	1	5
1. Islands of Meaning			
Chunks of Space	2	1.5	1.5
Blocks of Time	2	1.5	1.5
Frames	4	2	2
Chunks of Identity	2	2	1
Mental Fields	5	1.5	3.5
Ritual Transitions	5	2	2.5
2. The Great Divide			
Mental Gaps	4	1.5	3
Mental Quantum Leaps	5	1.5	3.5
Mental Images and Social Reality	7	1	7
3. The Rigid Mind			
Purity and Order	5	2.5	2
Self and Environment	3	2	1.5
Social Segregation	11	2	5.5
The Psychological Roots of Rigidity	6	1.5	4
Rigid Social Environments	13	2.5	5.5

Estimating how long it will take to write a manuscript *(continued)*

Section	Length (pages)	Pace (pages per day)	Time (days)
4. The Social Lens			
Culture and Classification	12	2	6
The Color Gray	6	1.5	4
The Social Construction of Discontinuity	8	1.5	5.5
5. The Fuzzy Mind			
The Ocean	7	1.5	5
Letting Go	2	1.5	1.5
Opening Up	2	1.5	1.5
Ritual Fluidity	2	2	1
Playful Promiscuity	4	2	2
Comic Transgression	4	2	2
Fluidity in Art	5	2	2.5
The Ethics of Fluidity	3	2.5	1.5
Fluidity and Modernity	12	2	6
6. The Flexible Mind			
Transgression and Creativity	3	1.5	2
Boundaries and Order	3	1	3
Mental Plasticity	5	1	5

eliminating all the days on which you will most probably *not* be able to write. You can now delineate your actual writing time by explicitly acknowledging the various constraints in your life that prevent you from being just a writer.

Everything you considered earlier when designing your regular weekly writing schedule should now be taken into account once again as you cross off your calendar all the days on which other commitments and obligations that you either cannot or are not willing to compromise (job, family) are likely to prevent you from doing any intensive writing. You also need to eliminate now any other days on which you are probably not going to be able to write—the days in the middle and at the end of the semester when you will have to grade a large number of papers and examinations in a rather short period of time, days when you plan to be out of town at conferences, days when schools are closed and your children stay home, the time when you plan to go away on vacation, the couple of weeks right before and after moving into a new house or apartment, the first few months after having a new baby, days on which you are going to have out-of-town guests staying over, and so on. Try to make sure that you actually eliminate *all* the days on which you are probably not going to be able to do any writing so as to avoid any future "surprises" and "last-minute complications" that could have been anticipated and avoided well in advance.

Once again, remember to overestimate the amount of work you have to do and underestimate your ability to do it. The more you do so, the better chance you will have later to actually meet your deadlines.

Thus, try to build into your timetable a few extra days beyond what you have already projected for each constituent segment of your manuscript. Like a shock absorber, such "slack time" will allow your timetable to withstand unexpected crises, as when you suddenly get sick or have to change jobs.[14] When writing *East of Eden*, John Steinbeck calculated thus: "I started active work on Feb. 19 so it is just

𝒥f you are facing an inflexible external deadline, set a slightly earlier one to avoid unnecessary pressure later, as you begin to approach it.

a little over two months. At that rate the book should only take 8 months and should be done by the first of November, but that is allowing for no accidents whatever and it would be an odd year when something drastic did not happen. *I am allowing two months for accidents* and will figure to be done by Christmas."[15]

For the very same reason, whenever you are facing a somewhat inflexible external deadline try to set for yourself a slightly *earlier* one to avoid unnecessary pressure later, as you begin to approach it. For example, if you absolutely must complete the second draft of your dissertation by April 15 in order to get some feedback from your advisor, who is going to be away all summer, try to actually have it ready by, say, March 25. Giving yourself such a three-week "safety cushion" will allow you to still be on time even if various unanticipated complications do arise.

Having estimated the amount of time you will need to write the various constituent segments of your manuscript

and also considered some of the problems you might anticipate along the way, you can now add one final column to
your timetable—a list of projected deadlines for the completion of each of those segments. Thus, if I plan to start working
on the third draft of my manuscript as soon as the spring
semester ends and to keep writing regularly every single
weekday during my summer and winter breaks (except for
the last three weeks of August, when I plan to go to a conference and then travel with my family) and on Tuesdays,
Thursdays, and Fridays during the fall semester, I can design
my final timetable (see the boxed example on pp. 76–77).

Notice that in order to reduce the amount of pressure I
may experience later I also count half days as full days when
I project my deadlines. For example, not only do I assign the
section "The Ethics of Fluidity" a day and a half instead of
only one day (despite the fact that writing three pages at a
pace of two and a half pages a day should take only about a
day), I also count that day and a half as two full working
days. That, along with the extra day of "slack time" I allow
for each section and the fact that during the fall semester I
can only write on Tuesdays, Thursdays, and Fridays, accounts
for the seven calendar days (December 3 through December
9) allotted to that "one-and-a-half-day section" on my timetable.

Based on such projections, I can now expect to complete
the third draft of my manuscript by January 12, 2000. (I can
also quite confidently commit myself to present at the conference I will attend in mid-August a paper based on the
section "Mental Images and Social Reality," which I expect to
finish by the end of June.) And unlike the deadlines authors
often set for themselves somewhat arbitrarily when planning

their graduation or signing advance book contracts, this is one on which I have good reason to believe that I can count.

While you are still working on any given draft of your manuscript, you can already start designing the timetable for the next one. In fact, as I have quite successfully managed to do with my books *Hidden Rhythms, Terra Cognita,* and *Social Mindscapes,* for which I had actually signed advance contracts before I even began working on my first draft, you can even project rather accurately when you might complete the entire manuscript, which is something you often need to do when you apply for a dissertation fellowship or sign an advance contract for a book. Before you can effectively do that, however, you also need to take into account the time *between* any two successive drafts of your manuscript.

Writing a dissertation or a book (and to a somewhat lesser extent a thesis) is an exhausting task, and you may need to take some time off occasionally. Try to build into your project timetable some periods of complete rest from writing between drafts to give yourself an opportunity to get away from your manuscript from time to time. It will also allow you to approach each draft with a somewhat fresh eye,[16] which is much more difficult to do when you are in the middle of writing it.

Leaving some time between drafts also gives you a chance to collect more data or to do some additional reading before you start working on your next draft (although reading is generally something I suggest you do *within* each draft during B-time stretches when you cannot do any intensive writing anyway). It also allows you to show your manuscript to your editor, thesis advisor, dissertation committee, or various colleagues and get some feedback on what you have written so

Estimating when you will finish writing a manuscript

Section	Length (pages)	Pace (pages per day)	Time (days)	Deadline
Introduction	5	1	5	5/10/99
1. Islands of Meaning				
Chunks of Space	2	1.5	1.5	5/13/99
Blocks of Time	2	1.5	1.5	5/18/99
Frames	4	2	2	5/21/99
Chunks of Identity	2	2	1	5/25/99
Mental Fields	5	1.5	3.5	6/1/99
Ritual Transitions	5	2	2.5	6/7/99
2. The Great Divide				
Mental Gaps	4	1.5	3	6/11/99
Mental Quantum Leaps	5	1.5	3.5	6/18/99
Mental Images and Social Reality	7	1	7	6/30/99
3. The Rigid Mind				
Purity and Order	5	2.5	2	7/5/99
Self and Environment	3	2	1.5	7/8/99
Social Segregation	11	2	5.5	7/19/99
The Psychological Roots of Rigidity	6	1.5	4	7/26/99
Rigid Social Environments	13	2.5	5.5	8/4/99

Estimating when you will finish writing a manuscript *(continued)*

Section	Length (pages)	Pace (pages per day)	Time (days)	Deadline
4. The Social Lens				
Culture and Classification	12	2	6	9/7/99
The Color Gray	6	1.5	4	9/17/99
The Social Construction of Discontinuity	8	1.5	5.5	10/5/99
5. The Fuzzy Mind				
The Ocean	7	1.5	5	10/21/99
Letting Go	2	1.5	1.5	10/28/99
Opening Up	2	1.5	1.5	11/4/99
Ritual Fluidity	2	2	1	11/9/99
Playful Promiscuity	4	2	2	11/16/99
Comic Transgression	4	2	2	11/23/99
Fluidity in Art	5	2	2.5	12/2/99
The Ethics of Fluidity	3	2.5	1.5	12/9/99
Fluidity and Modernity	12	2	6	12/24/99
6. The Flexible Mind				
Transgression and Creativity	3	1.5	2	12/29/99
Boundaries and Order	3	1	3	1/4/00
Mental Plasticity	5	1	5	1/12/00

far. It is important to do this between early drafts, when you are still open to suggestions and are willing to incorporate them into your manuscript. At the same time, however, unless those "pre-readers" are particularly supportive, you should also avoid collecting feedback too early, when you are still somewhat insecure about your project and unable to respond to criticism. That is why I usually circulate my manuscripts between the second and third drafts, when I have already completed two full drafts yet still have a couple more to go. For the same reason, it is usually my third drafts that I submit for publication, which allows me to present a pretty advanced version of my entire manuscript yet still have the opportunity to incorporate some useful substantive and editorial suggestions into my fourth and final draft.

To ensure that you get your pre-readers' feedback before you start working on your next draft, you need to contact them well in advance. Thus, if you are planning to finish the current draft of your dissertation by mid-October and start working on the next one in early December, try to alert your committee sometime around the second week of September that they should be expecting an approximately 240-page manuscript in about a month and that you would very much appreciate getting their feedback by mid-November (to be on the safe side). Needless to say, when you give people such ample lead time[17] (which you can only do, of course, when you are writing in accordance with an effective timetable and are constantly monitoring your progress), they are much more likely to be cooperative and try to accommodate your plans than if you were to suddenly dump such a long manuscript on their desk out of the blue and expect them to read it by next week.

Although setting deadlines, as I have tried to show here, is usually the very last step in the process of designing a timetable, there are many situations that nevertheless require you to actually begin this process by setting the deadline for the completion of your project and then plan everything else based on that. That was the kind of situation I faced when I decided to try to finish my dissertation before starting my first full-time job in September 1976, rightly suspecting that any "net" month of work left unfinished at that point might later take me a whole year to complete, as many doctoral students indeed discover. Years later I faced a similar situation with my book *Terra Cognita,* which dealt with the European "discovery" of America in 1492, when I had to base my entire planning on the fact that my publisher needed to have my manuscript ready by January 1992 in order to be able to publish it on the five-hundredth anniversary of that event nine months later.

Such situations, in fact, are not that unusual. Consider those instances when you need to have a substantial part of your dissertation ready by September 1999, since some of the teaching positions to which you plan to apply for the following academic year have an October deadline for sending all the supporting material, or when you absolutely need to finish your book by November 2002, when you are scheduled to come up for tenure. Consider also, along these lines, situations when you need to complete your thesis at least two or three weeks before your baby is due (to be on the safe side) or before your advisor is scheduled to leave for a one-year sabbatical leave abroad.

These are all situations where you need to adapt your timetable to various external constraints over which you have no control. To do so, take the deadline for the completion of your project as your starting point and base the pace at which you plan to be writing on that rather than the other way around. This kind of "backward" planning is not unlike trying to calculate the time for which you need to set your alarm in order to get to work on time. And just as you may have to eat your breakfast a little faster if you want to avoid having to get up before 7:00, you may also need to accelerate the pace at which you plan to write the third draft of your dissertation or book in order to meet your deadline. Needless to say, that too presupposes working in accordance with an effective timetable.

The Mechanics of Progress

In order to be able to use your writing schedule as well as project timetable most effectively, you also need to address the more mechanical aspects of the process of writing a thesis, dissertation, or book. Let me conclude by trying to examine some of them.

Getting Started

The first thing you need to do in order to write a thesis, dissertation, or book is produce a first draft. Indeed, writing a first draft is what "separates thousands of people who want to write a book from the few who actually do write books."[1]

The first draft of a manuscript, which is where we basically transform a set of often-disjointed ideas into a single coherent narrative, is almost inevitably going to be somewhat flawed. It is very important, therefore, that you treat your first drafts with kid gloves and accept the fact that they will most likely end up looking far from perfect. (Not that anybody else's first drafts look any better, as evident from the rather crude sketched "studies" produced by even the most famous artists at the early stages of working on their great masterpieces.) Furthermore, there is no reason why you should even show them to anyone. Although I usually circulate drafts of manuscripts on which I am working among friends and colleagues to get some feedback, I almost never show my very first drafts, which certainly helps me write them in a much less inhibited manner.

Yet very often we ourselves are our most critical and therefore inhibiting audience. At this stage of your project, when you are obviously much more vulnerable, it is therefore critical to avoid any self-censoring. After all, your first draft is also "the most uncertain—where you need guts, the ability to accept the imperfect until it is better."[2] And since you are basically working with clay rather than marble[3] and will have ample opportunity later to further improve what you are writing, you can afford to write your first draft in a somewhat more relaxed manner. As John Steinbeck once advised writers who are working on their first drafts, "Write freely and as rapidly as possible and throw the whole thing on paper. Never correct or rewrite until the whole thing is down. Rewrite in process is usually found to be an excuse for not going on."[4]

Moving Along

A major problem with which you inevitably need to grapple as a writer is how to make your writing more "linear." Unlike routine activities such as grocery shopping or making your bed in the morning, there is a critical cumulative dimension to the process of producing a manuscript. The challenge, of course, is to make sure that your writing moves in a linear fashion rather than "in circles," so that you indeed end up with a fully completed thesis, dissertation, or book rather than standing in one place and just spinning your wheels.

At the level of the writing session, your main task is to ensure that, in marked contrast to essentially "circular" activities such as cleaning your kitchen or doing your laundry, when you sit down tomorrow to write you will not find yourself at the same point in your manuscript where you were yesterday. In other words, you need to keep "moving along."

The first thing I do to avoid writing in circles is to practically never begin a writing session by reviewing what I wrote in the last one. This rather common, seemingly innocuous practice actually draws on our deepest insecurities as writers (those that hinder our ability to "let go" of our ideas), thereby often serving as a well-disguised excuse for procrastinating.

In order to avoid this trap, however, you must tighten the link between any given writing session and the previous one[5] so as to allow yourself to "enter" it with somewhat less effort. Especially given the need to make sure that you do not lose any "momentum" between them, you must be able to begin your sessions by picking up right where you left the last time.

To prevent myself from spending too much time warming up, I end my sessions by doing some "prepping" for the following ones. I thus try not to stretch my actual writing until the very end of the session, usually stopping when I am still "in top form," and use the remaining time, when I am somewhat more tired and less creative, for making all the necessary "B-time" preparations for the next session. Like surgical staff

preparing for an operation, I try to gather everything I believe
I will need the next time I sit down to write, and also start
editing the last draft of the next couple of pages in my manuscript (using my estimated pace of progress as a guide for
projecting how many). Sections I have already started editing
will require less work, which is why even on "bad" days when
I fail to make much progress in my actual writing I nevertheless still try to do such "pre-writing" so as to allow myself
a somewhat easier entry into my next session. On a large
easel-like bulletin board standing by my side on a tripod I
then display those half-edited pages along with all the related
ideas I have generated, readings I have done, and new data I
have collected since having written my last draft. I arrange
all this material in visually distinct clusters that correspond
to what I intend to be my new paragraphs, with the actual
spaces between them essentially representing the mental
spaces separating those paragraphs from one another in my
mind.[6] Thus, the next time I sit down to work, I can actually
see before me quite clearly both the content and the structure
of what I plan to write that day.

In an effort to further resist the tendency to procrastinate
by writing in circles, I also try to make sure that I am indeed
moving along by writing each new draft of any given segment
of my manuscript in an altogether different computer file
than the previous draft. (I retype my entire manuscript from
start to finish each draft, thereby making sure that at no point
during the process of producing it do I ever pass over a sentence without rethinking it. In fact, even when I am working
on the very final draft I still make active decisions about every
single sentence in it.) When I am writing the third draft of a
particular section of my manuscript, for example, I thus work

with three different documents simultaneously—(a) the old, second-draft version of that section, (b) the new, third-draft version that I am in the process of creating, and (c) a "working draft" file that I use as a sort of shuttle service between them. I thus import a paragraph from the old, second-draft version (unless I am creating a brand new paragraph) into the "working draft" file, do all my revising there, and then literally transport the revised paragraph to the new, third-draft file when I am ready to move on to the next paragraph. When "saving" these files, I also avoid mishaps by labeling them in a manner that clearly indicates which drafts they represent.

During the entire process of revising, I also try to enhance my experience of actual "movement" by constantly shifting between two somewhat different modes of writing. I usually begin this process by incorporating all the ideas I have generated, readings I have done, and new data I have collected since having written the last draft into the old, second-draft version of that paragraph, transporting it into my "working draft" file, doing some rough editing there, and then printing out a hard copy of the semi-revised paragraph. I then literally move into another chair (so as to substantiate my experience of moving along) and edit that paragraph by hand. I then transfer all the changes I have made in the text to my "working draft" file and do some further revising there. I keep doing this for several rounds until I am finally ready to move on to the next paragraph.

Closing

Before I can actually move on to the next paragraph, however, I need to be able to put the one I have just finished revising behind me. In order to do that (and ultimately not feel the urge to begin every work session by "reviewing" what I wrote in the previous one), I need to regard the new version of that paragraph as final at least until the next draft.

To enhance the sense of finality I wish to infuse into the new version of segments I revise, I try to introduce some closure into my writing. Thus, when revising text, I literally "move" (rather than merely "copy") it from the old document to my "working draft" file and ultimately to the new document, virtually deleting the old version of every paragraph I revise while regarding its new version as closed until the next draft. At the end of every work session, I also make sure that I save the new document including everything I have managed to "close" that day on my hard drive as well as back it up on three or four separate diskettes in case I ever lose my electronic grip and start falling off the mental mountain I am trying to climb.

To further convince myself that I can actually "let go" and move on to the next paragraph, I also print out a hard copy of every new paragraph I "close" on a special high-quality paper in order to help me regard it at least for the time being as final until the next draft. Such tangible evidence also helps me appreciate the realness of what I am producing in a world that is rapidly becoming comfortable with the once-inconceivable idea of essentially virtual text. After all, stacking all my "closed," consecutively numbered pages together in an ever-growing pile allows me to actually *see* how all those tiny grains of mental sand add up to real mountains! Indeed, it is the ability to visualize this cumulative, "linear" nature of my writing that allows me to experience the progress I am constantly making on my manuscript.

Achieving closure is critical not only at the level of the writing session but also at major junctures in your manuscript. Thus, just as you may want to mark the conclusion of a session by printing out a hard copy of what you have produced so as to reaffirm to yourself that it is in fact "closed," you may also want to mark the completion of each draft of a chapter (not to mention entire drafts) of your manuscript by some ritual celebration. Like weddings, graduation ceremonies, and other rites of passage specifically designed to help substantiate crossings of critical mental thresholds,[7] it will add a certain sense of finality to what you "close" and thus protect you from the nagging urge to keep revising it even before you get to revisit it on your next draft. If accompanied by a symbolic "treat" such as a special dinner, it will also serve as a celebratory reward for your accomplishment.

Along similar lines, you also need to achieve closure at the level of your manuscript as a whole. Working on any given project for too long can generate serious problems. Aside from the philosophical question of whether, as Anthony Burgess put it, "the writer can be the same person . . . over a long stretch of time,"[8] there is also the psychological problem that what may have once been a source of great pleasure and excitement can become a source of boredom and frustration, and writers who have been working on the same manuscript for too long often reach a point when they actually come to hate it. Thus, just as you need to learn to end your work sessions before you reach the point when your writing is no longer effective, you also need to be careful not to reach a point when you may burn out and become totally fed up with your project.

The problem, unfortunately, is that we often have difficulty letting go of our projects and bringing them to completion, a difficulty typically manifested in the perfectionist urge to keep revising our manuscripts over and over. Such perfectionism (also expressed in the compulsive urge to read everything possibly related to our project) may lead us to keep spinning our intellectual wheels and work on the same project indefinitely.

Setting firm deadlines for completion is the single most effective way of closing essentially open-ended tasks.

The best way to resist our perfectionism is by using deadlines. Setting firm deadlines for completion is the single most effective way of "closing" essentially open-ended tasks that lack inherent limits.[9] As such, it helps counteract the effects of Parkinson's Law, whereby work typically expands to fill the time available for its completion.[10]

Students who ask their professors for extensions on their term papers may not realize that, except in extreme situations such as after having undergone major surgery or losing a parent, those who are willing to give them an "Incomplete" grade are actually not helping them at all. In fact, they help them trap themselves in a vicious procrastinatory circle that only prolongs the process of completing their assignments, sometimes indefinitely.

Despite their unfortunate lethal etymology, deadlines offer the best way out of such a vicious circle. Setting a firm deadline for completion is the most effective way to put a necessary stop to what may otherwise become an endless Sisyphean ordeal. We should therefore learn to utilize those extremely helpful devices even when we are not forced by others (professors, publishers) to do so. By helping solve the problem of indefinitely receding horizons, deadlines are among a writer's best friends.

Storage and Retrieval

Part of what makes it somewhat easier for me to go ahead and "close" any given segment of my manuscript is the knowledge that just because I may not actively keep revising it for several months does not mean that I stop working on it altogether. That implies, of course, that I can still keep generating ideas as well as collecting data that I may later incorporate into that segment when I get to revisit it on my next draft.

The relatively long time separating any two consecutive drafts of any given segment of your manuscript, however, certainly requires you to carefully preserve all the material that you manage to generate between them and make sure that it will not be forgotten or lost by the next time you get to work on that segment. That, of course, implies the need to consider how you store your ideas as well as retrieve them.

It is extremely important, for example, that you put your new ideas in writing,[11] whether on the margins of the most current draft of your manuscript or as separate notes that can be attached to or at least stored (either physically or electronically) along with it. To avoid ever losing what could have been a great idea, you need to get into the habit of writing down your ideas as soon as you have them (which also implies having to keep a lot of pens and notepads around you, including in your car and on your nightstand, since you can never tell in advance when or where they might strike you). If you consistently keep a record of these thoughts, you will be quite amazed to discover by the time you get to your next draft how many new ideas you have actually generated in the meantime.

When you write down your ideas, try not to worry about the possibility that you may encounter some redundancy later, when you start working on your next draft and reexamining everything you have accumulated since the last one. After all, it is better to write down the same idea three times than to lose it altogether just because you assume that you already wrote it down several months earlier. It is quite possible, for example, that what you wrote down back then was slightly different, and that the new nuance you are now introducing can in fact make that entire section of your manuscript much richer or clearer.

For the same reason, it may also be extremely useful to write down brief accounts of how you present your project (or particular parts of it) to others right after talking with them. Since different people usually take different aspects of our work for granted, we normally tend to highlight different things in our projects to different audiences. Thus, if you write down brief accounts of how you presented a particular chapter of your dissertation on three separate occasions, for example, you may actually discover later upon reexamining them that they are perhaps not as identical as they may have originally seemed to you, and that having those three different versions side by side in front of you can in fact help you make your argument much richer, stronger, sharper, or clearer the next time you get to work on that chapter.

Indeed, all this also applies to the preliminary stage before you even begin to write your manuscript. Even first drafts are rarely written entirely from scratch. As Bernard Malamud once put it, "when I start [to write] I have a pretty well developed idea what the book is about and how it ought to go, because generally I've been thinking about it and making notes for months if not years."[12] Joseph Heller's *Catch 22* preliminary card file, in fact, was the size of a shoebox.[13] In other words, although the actual writing may just begin, ideas as well as data may have been accumulating for years. I still recall my initial shock sixteen years ago when, after having spent a full day going through a pile of notes and memos I had been filing sporadically for a couple of years for a short article I intended to write on the seven-day week as a social institution, it suddenly dawned on me that over the course of those two years I had actually laid out the foundations of what would soon become the first draft of a full-fledged book (*The Seven-Day Circle*)! By the same token, although I technically have not begun writing my next book (on the social structure of the past), I have in fact been filing copious preliminary notes on that subject for the past fourteen years.

Along with all the data I collect, the notes I take when I read something related to the topic I am writing about, the already-"closed" sections of the most current draft of my manuscript, and the yet-to-be-revised sections of the last one, I usually store the ideas I generate in plastic color-coded mini-drawers representing the various stairs leading to the top of the mental mountain I am presently trying to climb. Since spatial (and particularly visual) compartmentalization helps substantiate mental compartmentalization,[14] I basically assign each distinct section in my manuscript a separate drawer, and each cluster of drawers representing a distinct chapter a separate color. Thus, if I am working on a book that has seven chapters subdivided into twenty-six sections, for example, I arrange on my desk a set of twenty-six such intellectual containers unambiguously organized in seven distinctly color-coded clusters.

Although I could easily achieve the same level of textual organization by creating seven separate directories subdivided into twenty-six distinct subdirectories on my computer, it would certainly never allow me what this system does, which is to actually *see* the entire outline of my book in front of me while I am writing it! The importance of being able to do so can hardly be overstated. Throughout the several months or years that you work on your manuscript you will need to constantly keep thinking about it in terms of its various constituent segments. Then you will know instantly where to store new ideas you develop or data you collect and be able to successfully retrieve them later. Whether it is in the form of a virtual memo electronically "saved" somewhere on your hard disk or an actual three-by-five index card lying in a drawer or folder, you must be able to access it right away when you need it. Otherwise, even the most important ideas and data you may have developed and collected would be totally useless for all practical purposes. Needless to say, the threat of actually losing or forgetting things we have already discovered or thought about is endemic to the unusually long process of producing manuscripts such as theses, dissertations, and books and calls for an effective system of retrieval.

Given all that, it is extremely important that you learn to

think about your manuscript in terms of its various constituent building blocks (chapters as well as distinct sections within chapters). And it is certainly much easier to do so when you are able to see its overall structure in front of you while you are writing it.

For the same reason, before I actually start revising any given chapter in my manuscript I often try to reacquaint myself with its overall structure by making a list of one-line synopses of each of its various constituent paragraphs. That usually allows me to see the general outline of that entire chapter on a single page, which makes it much easier for me to notice various redundancies I may not have noticed earlier in the text as well as to try to make the chapter "flow" somewhat better by essentially altering the way its various segments are sequentially arranged vis-a-vis one another.

Road Maps and Benchmarks

Writing in a linear fashion almost calls for some graphic articulation of your plans, a sort of road map[15] on which you can actually chart the general course you have set for yourself as well as various benchmarks along the way to help you monitor your progress periodically.[16] Like a seasoned traveler, you can basically visualize on such a chart every single step of your project over the next several months or years as well as the actual progress you are constantly making on it.

The more easily accessible such a chart is, the more likely you are to use it. It is extremely useful, therefore, to have on your desk or your computer a copy of your project timetable, listing the various constituent segments of the manuscript on which you are currently working and projecting for each of those segments its approximate length, the pace at which you plan to write it, the amount of time you estimate you will need for writing it, and a tentative deadline for its completion.

For short-term planning and navigation, however, I also hang on the wall of my study a calendar on which I super-impose the more immediate parts of this master plan. The calendar I use for this purpose is an erasable, plastic-surface two-by-three-foot four-month planner that you can get at any stationery store. I especially like this particular kind of calendar because I find four months to be a perfect time framework for doing short-term planning on my manuscripts. Not only is it a convenient length, it also roughly corresponds to some relatively homogeneous seasons in my daily professional life as an academic, namely the fall (from September through December) and spring (from January through April) semesters and the summer (from May through August). Each of those three four-month blocks has a rather distinctive temporal profile in terms of the various constraints imposed on my regular weekly writing schedule. As such, it provides an ideal context for doing all my short-term planning.

On this planner I first identify the days on which I plan to be working on my manuscript. Once again, I begin by eliminating all the days on which I will most probably *not* be able to do any manuscript-related writing during the four-month period represented on the calendar. I thus first cross out the days of the week on which I either cannot or am not willing to do any intensive writing on a regular basis (Mondays and Wednesdays, which are particularly busy days for me at school, as well as Saturdays, on which I usually like to take a break from my work). I also cross out at this point any days on which I will most likely have only a very short time for writing. However, if those are days on which I can definitely anticipate writing sessions that would be at least half as long as my regular ones, I count them as half-days and expect to complete one half of my projected daily quota for that particular segment of my manuscript. Next, I cross out any other days on which I do not plan to be doing any writing during this coming "season" (the weeks in the middle and at the end of the semester when I expect to be busy grading papers and exams, holidays I wish to spend with my family, a two-day conference out of town, days of special meetings at the university which I have to attend). Having done that, I then mark with color-coded stickers all the remaining days that I designate as "writing days" yet on which I must work on various projects other than my manuscript (a paper I am writing for a journal, a special lecture I have been invited to give, my presentation at a conference, a book review). The days that "survive" those three rounds of elimination I then mark with red stickers (or half-stickers for half-days). Those are the days on which I plan to be working on my manuscript. Having done all that, I also mark on this calendar my projected deadlines for the conclusion of any section, chapter, or entire draft of my manuscript that I plan to complete during this coming "season."

Being able to visualize your writing plans in such tremendous detail certainly helps to demystify them. After all, seeing your entire next semester laid out so clearly before you offers you a much more realistic picture of what you can actually expect from yourself during this period. It thus helps to make the entire process of projecting your progress much more predictable and therefore also less intimidating.

Having designed such a remarkable "road map," however, you also need to make sure that you actually look at it from time to time in order to monitor the progress you are making on your manuscript. Like pilots and navigators who keep referring to their charts to determine their current location and compare it to where they should be according to their projections, you need to develop a habit of glancing at this seasonal calendar periodically in order to compare where you actually are in your manuscript to where you should be according to your project timetable and thus find out whether you are indeed on, ahead of, or behind schedule. That is why it is so important to have both your timetable and this planner readily available for frequent scrutiny. Such constant feedback will certainly help prevent otherwise unavoidable unpleasant surprises such as suddenly realizing, for example, that you are still eight full working days away from completing a particular section of your manuscript that you are scheduled to present in three days at a conference.

Discipline and Flexibility

And yet, like any seasoned traveler, you also need to develop a certain amount of flexibility in order to be able to adapt your plans to changing circumstances,[17] so that your entire structure does not collapse whenever anything goes wrong. Thus, when you suddenly notice that you are a few days behind schedule, you can always make some slight adjustments in your timetable (pick up the pace, work longer hours) to correct the situation. And if your writing is unexpectedly interrupted for a couple of weeks by some emergency in your family or when you suddenly have to move and start a new job, you certainly ought to be able to readjust your plans accordingly.

At the same time, however, you should also try not to tamper with your timetables and schedules *too* often. Everything I have suggested in this book can only work effectively if you develop at least some commitment to the various routines, plans, and deadlines you set for yourself. It will be utterly useless if you do not.

· ·

It requires a lot of self-discipline to be ready to write whether you feel particularly inspired or not.

· ·

That is why it is so important that you deliberately overestimate the magnitude of your project while at the same time underestimating the pace at which you expect to be working on it, thereby building into your general plan some shock absorbers that can help you overcome unexpected problems without having to keep readjusting your timetable every couple of days. Yet you also need to develop some self-discipline. It requires a lot of self-discipline to regard your regular writing schedule as sacred[18] and always be ready to write on certain days and at certain times whether you feel particularly "inspired" or not. It also requires a lot of self-discipline to stick to your deadlines once you are no longer in school and therefore need to impose them on yourself. Indeed, you may soon discover that you actually miss not having around you those "inconsiderate" professors who always forced you to hand in your papers by a certain date no matter what.

The very notion of a "clockwork muse" may sound somewhat oxymoronic at first given the way we normally associate creativity with spontaneity. It certainly goes against our traditional romantic image of a writer as someone who forgoes structure in order to accommodate essentially unscheduled outbursts of creative energy. Yet only those who develop a certain amount of self-discipline actually end up completing theses, dissertations, and books. And you need to do that in order to become an author of one.

.

Notes · Index

Notes

1. The Clockwork Muse

1. See Eviatar Zerubavel, *Hidden Rhythms: Schedules and Calendars in Social Life* (Berkeley: University of California Press, 1985 [1981]), pp. 31–69.
2. See ibid., pp. 44–49. See also Michel Foucault, *Discipline and Punish: The Birth of the Prison* (New York: Vintage, 1979 [1975]), pp. 149–162.
3. See Zerubavel, *Hidden Rhythms*, pp. 59–64.
4. See also Eviatar Zerubavel, "The Language of Time: Towards a Semiotics of Temporality," *Sociological Quarterly* 28 (1987): 344.
5. See also Zerubavel, *Hidden Rhythms*, pp. 51–54; Eviatar Zerubavel, *The Seven-Day Circle: The History and Meaning of the Week* (Chicago: University of Chicago Press, 1989 [1985]), pp. 103–106.
6. On the segregative function of time, see also Zerubavel, *Hidden Rhythms*, pp. 101–166.

7. John Barth, *The Friday Book: Essays and Other Nonfiction* (New York: G. P. Putnam's Sons, 1984), p. xii.
8. See also Daniel F. Chambliss, "The Mundanity of Excellence: An Ethnographic Report on Stratification and Olympic Swimmers," *Sociological Theory* 7 (1988): 70–87.
9. On the modern utilitarian approach to time, see Zerubavel, *Hidden Rhythms*, pp. 54–59. See also Staffan B. Linder, *The Harried Leisure Class* (New York: Columbia University Press, 1970).

2. The Writing Schedule

1. Zerubavel, *Hidden Rhythms*, pp. 31–40.
2. See Zerubavel, *The Seven-Day Circle*, pp. 86–106.
3. On the inevitable tension between personal choices and various external constraints, see Kathleen Gerson, *Hard Choices: How Women Decide about Work, Career, and Motherhood* (Berkeley: University of California Press, 1985); Kathleen Gerson, *No Man's Land: Men's Changing Commitments to Family and Work* (New York: Basic Books, 1993).
4. See also Christena Nippert-Eng, *Home and Work: Negotiating Boundaries through Everyday Life* (Chicago: University of Chicago Press, 1996), pp. 152–228.
5. "The Art of Fiction—Ernest Hemingway," *The Paris Review* 18 (1958): 66.
6. "The Art of Fiction—John Irving," *The Paris Review* 100 (1986): 77.
7. "The Art of Fiction—Henry Miller," *The Paris Review* 28 (1962): 131; "The Art of Fiction—Gore Vidal," *The Paris Review* 59 (1974): 157; "The Art of Fiction—John Updike," *The Paris Review* 45 (1968): 96; "The Art of Fiction—William Styron," *The Paris Review* 5 (1954): 46; "The Art of Fiction—

Cynthia Ozick," *The Paris Review* 102 (1986): 157; "The Art of Fiction—Mario Vargas Llosa," *The Paris Review* 116 (1990): 57; "The Art of Fiction—John Dos Passos," *The Paris Review* 46 (1969): 165; "The Art of Fiction—Carlos Fuentes," *The Paris Review* 82 (1981): 144; a radio interview with John Grisham on *Fresh Air,* National Public Radio, May 23, 1997; "The Art of Fiction—Maya Angelou," *The Paris Review* 116 (1990): 149.

8. See also Zerubavel, *The Seven-Day Circle,* pp. 90–91.
9. "The Art of Fiction—Gabriel Garcia Marquez," *The Paris Review* 82 (1981): 63.
10. Zerubavel, *Hidden Rhythms,* pp. 1–12, 40–44.
11. "The Art of Fiction—Toni Morrison," *The Paris Review* 128 (1993): 86.
12. "The Art of Fiction: Henry Miller," p. 131.
13. "The Art of Fiction: Anthony Burgess," *The Paris Review* 56 (1973):121.
14. "The Art of Fiction: James Baldwin," *The Paris Review* 91 (1984): 66–67.
15. "The Art of Fiction: Mario Vargas Llosa," p. 57.
16. Viriginia Woolf, *A Room of One's Own* (San Diego: Harcourt Brace Jovanovich, 1957 [1929]), pp. 109–110.
17. See, for example, "The Art of Fiction—Mario Vargas Llosa," p. 58.
18. "The Art of Fiction—Maya Angelou," p. 149. Consider also, in this regard, the character played by Gena Rowlands in Woody Allen's 1988 film *Another Woman.*
19. On "private time," see Zerubavel, *Hidden Rhythms,* pp. 138–166.
20. "The Art of Fiction—Ernest Hemingway," p. 65.
21. "The Art of Fiction—Anthony Burgess," pp. 121–122.
22. "The Art of Fiction—Tom Stoppard," *The Paris Review* 109

(1988): 41. See also "The Art of Fiction—James Baldwin," pp. 66–67.

23. "The Art of Fiction—Toni Morrison," p. 86. See also Christena Nippert-Eng, " 'Mommy, Mommy,' or 'Excuse Me, Ma'am': Gender and Interruptions at Home and Work" (paper presented at the annual meeting of the American Sociological Association, Pittsburgh, August 1992).

24. See also "The Art of Fiction—Gabriel Garcia Marquez," p. 63; "The Art of Fiction—Margaret Atwood," *The Paris Review* 117 (1990): 81.

25. See, for example, "The Art of Fiction—Anthony Burgess," p. 125.

26. See, for example, "The Art of Fiction—Françoise Sagan," *The Paris Review* 14 (1956): 85.

27. For more on this, see also Alan Lakein, *How To Get Control of Your Time and Your Life* (New York: Signet Books, 1973), pp. 28–29, 46–48.

28. See also ibid., pp. 52–59.

3. A Mountain with Stairs

1. On the fundamental difference between those two approaches to time, see, for example, Zerubavel, *The Seven-Day Circle,* pp. 83–86.

2. Eviatar Zerubavel, *The Fine Line: Making Distinctions in Everyday Life* (Chicago: University of Chicago Press, 1993 [1991]), pp. 61–80. See also Eviatar Zerubavel, "Language and Memory: 'Pre-Columbian' America and the Social Logic of Periodization," *Social Research* 65 (1998): 315–330.

3. On mental flexibility, see Zerubavel, *The Fine Line,* pp. 120–122.

4. See also ibid., pp. 118–119.

5. "The Art of Fiction—Alberto Moravia," *The Paris Review* 6 (1954): 29.

6. "The Art of Fiction—Bernard Malamud," *The Paris Review* 61 (1975): 48.

7. See also, in this regard, "The Art of Fiction—Truman Capote," *The Paris Review* 16 (1957): 46–48; "The Art of Fiction—Günter Grass," *The Paris Review* 119 (1991): 213.

8. Jacques Barzun, *On Writing, Editing, and Publishing: Essays Explicative and Hortatory* (2nd ed. Chicago: University of Chicago Press, 1986), p. 7.

9. Ibid.

10. "The Art of Fiction—Mario Vargas Llosa," p. 56. Emphasis added.

11. On the fundamental distinction between "gross" and "net" time, see Zerubavel, *Hidden Rhythms,* pp. 62–63.

4. The Project Timetable

1. Eviatar Zerubavel, *Patterns of Time in Hospital Life: A Sociological Perspective* (Chicago: University of Chicago Press, 1979), pp. 98–101; Zerubavel, *The Seven-Day Circle,* pp. 102–103.

2. "The Art of Fiction—Norman Mailer," *The Paris Review* 31 (1964): 33–35.

3. See, for example, "The Art of Fiction—Mario Vargas Llosa," p. 56.

4. See also "The Art of Fiction—Günter Grass," p. 214.

5. See also Joseph Horowitz, *Critical Path Scheduling: Management Control through CPM and PERT* (New York: Ronald Press, 1967), pp. 46–47.

6. See also Emile Durkheim, *Suicide: A Study in Sociology* (New York: Free Press, 1966 [1897]), pp. 247–276; Emile Durkheim,

Moral Education: A Study in the Theory and Application of the Sociology of Education (New York: Free Press, 1973 [1925]), pp. 39–46.

7. "The Art of Fiction—E. L. Doctorow," *The Paris Review* 101 (1986): 40.

8. "The Art of Fiction—Kingsley Amis," *The Paris Review* 64 (1975): 64.

9. See "The Art of Fiction—Graham Greene," *The Paris Review* 3 (1953): 36–37; Graham Greene, *Ways of Escape* (New York: Simon and Schuster, 1980), p. 92.

10. "The Art of Fiction—John Steinbeck," *The Paris Review* 48 (1969): 185. Emphasis added.

11. "The Art of Fiction—Philip Roth," *The Paris Review* 93 (1984): 218. See also Chambliss, "The Mundanity of Excellence."

12. Zerubavel, *Hidden Rhythms,* pp. 62–63.

13. See also Horowitz, *Critical Path Scheduling,* pp. 32, 71.

14. See also ibid., pp. 147–148; Lakein, *How to Get Control of Your Time and Your Life,* p. 51.

15. "The Art of Fiction—John Steinbeck," p. 185. Emphasis added.

16. See also "The Art of Fiction—Henry Miller," p. 133.

17. See also Zerubavel, "The Language of Time," p. 345.

5. The Mechanics of Progress

1. Kenneth Atchity, *A Writer's Time: A Guide to the Creative Process from Vision through Revision* (New York: W. W. Norton, 1986), p. 61.

2. "The Art of Fiction—Bernard Malamud," p. 48.

3. Barzun, *On Writing, Editing, and Publishing,* p. 8. See also "The Art of Fiction—Mario Vargas Llosa," p. 56.

4. "The Art of Fiction (Continued)—John Steinbeck," *The Paris Review* 63 (1975): 181. See also "The Art of Fiction—Gore Vidal," p. 157.

5. See also Atchity, *A Writer's Time*, pp. 41–43.
6. On the way we use actual physical partitions to substantiate mental partitions we wish to establish and preserve in our minds, see Zerubavel, *The Fine Line*, pp. 7–9, 22–23.
7. See Arnold Van Gennep, *The Rites of Passage* (Chicago: University of Chicago Press, 1960 [1909]); Zerubavel, *The Fine Line*, pp. 18–20.
8. "The Art of Fiction—Anthony Burgess," p. 125.
9. See also Zerubavel, *The Fine Line*, p. 119.
10. See C. Northcote Parkinson, *Parkinson's Law and Other Studies in Administration* (Boston: Houghton Mifflin, 1957), pp. 2–13.
11. On the role of writing in preserving memory, see, for example, Eviatar Zerubavel, *Social Mindscapes: An Invitation to Cognitive Sociology* (Cambridge, Mass.: Harvard University Press, 1997), p. 93.
12. "The Art of Fiction—Bernard Malamud," p. 57.
13. "The Art of Fiction—Joseph Heller," *The Paris Review* 60 (1974): 136.
14. Zerubavel, *The Fine Line*, pp. 7–9, 97–102, 108–110. On drawers, see also Gaston Bachelard, *The Poetics of Space* (Boston: Beacon Press, 1969 [1958]), p. 77.
15. See also Atchity, *A Writer's Time*, pp. 63–64.
16. For a general discussion of such benchmarks, see also Julius A. Roth, *Timetables: Structuring the Passage of Time in Hospital Treatment and Other Careers* (Indianapolis: Bobbs-Merrill, 1963).
17. See also Horowitz, *Critical Path Scheduling*, pp. 169–171.
18. See also "The Art of Fiction—Mario Vargas Llosa," p. 57.

Index